D1110028

PITCHMAN'S MELODY:
SHAW ABOUT "SHAKESPEAR"

PITCHMAN'S MELODY:
SHAW ABOUT "SHAKESPEAR"

Jerry Lutz

Lewisburg
BUCKNELL UNIVERSITY PRESS

Associated University Presses, Inc.
Cranbury, New Jersey 08512

Library of Congress Cataloging in Publication Data

Lutz, Jerry.
    Pitchman's melody: Shaw about "Shakespear".

    Bibliography: p.
    1. Shaw, George Bernard, 1856–1950. 2. Shakespeare,
William, 1564–1616. I. Title.
PR5367.L8 1974   822′.9′12   72-3529
ISBN 0-8387-1247-9

PRINTED IN THE UNITED STATES OF AMERICA

For my parents

Contents

Acknowledgments   9

1   Introduction   13
2   Putting Shakespeare to Use   17
3   Shaw's Principles of Criticism   35
4   Music and Thought: Shakespeare vs. Ibsen   57
5   Shakespearean Production   87
6   The Exposer Exposed   137

Notes   153
Bibliography   163
Index   169

Acknowledgments

A freshman at the University of Iowa, I took Ancient and Modern Literature, taught by Rhodes Dunlap. Stopping at his office was risky. He invariably suggested a paper topic. I remember one in particular: Shaw's criticism of Shakespeare.

For the Ph.D. thesis at Harvard, I had two other fine advisers: Harry Levin and William Alfred, who pushed me with their criticism and pulled me with their encouragement.

I thank all these. The Society of Authors, on behalf of the Bernard Shaw Estate, has granted permission to quote from Shaw's published works and to refer to his unpublished works. Reference to his unpublished works is also by permission of the Harvard College Library. The Trustees of Mrs. Patrick Campbell give permission to quote from *Bernard Shaw and Mrs. Patrick Campbell: Their Correspondence*. I have both quoted from and referred to unpublished works that Shaw did not write: by courtesy of the Victoria and Albert Museum, The Folger Shakespeare Library, and the Garrick Club.

I thank Miss Helen D. Willard, former Curator of the Harvard Theatre Collection.

Mark Freedman has shown me a sense of coherence and a sense of shape, how parts may—sometimes—form a whole.

Among C. D. Gaston's accomplishments are these: his interest in Shakespeare was demonstrated when he took my course at Kadena, Okinawa, and he designed the dust jacket for this book.

In revising, I had the aid of these sympathetic hardheads: Alan Cholodenko, Martha Fuller, Paul Hager, Keith Kester, Gary McCown, Carole Neville, Stanwood Piper, Prasun Sinha, Carol and Bill Wooten.

9

PITCHMAN'S MELODY:
SHAW ABOUT "SHAKESPEAR"

Shaw is both a fine word-musician and a pitchman advertising his wares.

1
Introduction

Shaw had fierce competition. English theaters neglected him but produced "Shakespear," as Shaw spelled it. To gain a name for himself, Shaw attacked Shakespeare. Necessarily prevented from self-defense, Shakespeare has survived in reasonably good health, and now the stage has room for both.

Shaw worked overtime to strengthen the rivalry (chapter 2, "Putting Shakespeare to Use"). In plays, reviews, letters, and essays, Shakespeare makes an appearance. He even becomes a character in two plays, *The Dark Lady of the Sonnets* and *Shakes Versus Shav*. Another play, *Cymbeline Refinished*, is Shaw's variation on Shakespeare's fifth act.

Shaw wrote most of his Shakespearean criticism in reviews and prefaces. He first reviewed music (*The Star* and *The World*, 1888–1894), then theater (*The Saturday Review*, 1895–1898). Shaw was an admirable theater reviewer because he analyzed both play and performance, the philosophical and the practical (chapter 3, "Shaw's Principles of Criticism"). Shaw had various interests in the theater—as playwright, propagandist, director, and collector of royalties. The theater was a necessary part of him, no more an excuse for rhapsodizing than his corpuscles and arteries.

Shaw's standards were individual, to say the least. Not every Shakespearean critic has announced his intention to be unfair. There are two extremes in considering this criticism: to dismiss it completely as so much hot air, or to kowtow to the opinions of a great author and assume that everything he says is, as a matter of course, lustrous and sensible. Shaw cannot be read with mouth turned down at the corners, although the first reaction to his reviews is often dismay or outrage. But Shaw aimed for an effect: to wake people up. What more efficient method than cold water?

Shaw objected to Shakespeare, but he had great praise for Ibsen (chapter 4, "Music and Thought: Shakespeare vs. Ibsen"). Shaw made a tricky approach; he claimed that Shakespeare, supreme as word-musician, could not match Ibsen as thinker and critic of religion and morality. Shaw complained that the Victorians played Shakespeare "with his brains cut out."[1] He rarely admitted that Shakespeare had any. How could anyone pay attention to that intellectual nullity while Ibsen waited in the wings? On the other hand, Shakespeare *was* the undisputed master composer of word music. Shaw's admiration, second to none, is suspect; he implies that the beauty of the music is directly proportional to the weakness of the thought.

In his valedictory to theater reviewing, Shaw says that "my reputation shall not suffer: it is built up fast and solid, like Shakespear's, on an impregnable basis of dogmatic reiteration."[2] There is a difference. Other people reiterated for Shakespeare; Shaw reiterated for himself. He sums up his reviewing achievements for the Bard: "When I began to write, William was a divinity and a bore. Now he is a fellow creature; and his plays have reached an unprecedented pitch of popularity. And yet his worshippers overwhelm my name with insult." Greater power hath no reviewer. It is debatable whether that unprecedented pitch of popularity had much to do with Shaw. Yet he had brought new energy to theater reviewing, which would not be quite the same again. For that matter, Shakespeare would not be quite the same again.

Shaw wrote his best criticism about staging Shakespeare (chapter 5, "Shakespearean Production"). Shaw's blood pressure was consistently raised by "Bardicide," practiced by Henry Irving at the Lyceum Theatre. Irving featured the pictorial style and cut large chunks of the text to make room for imposing scenic effects. This style gave the scene painter precedence over Shakespeare. As a playwright, Shaw was offended by these mutilations. Irving had no literary sense, for he produced blank-verse claptrap like Bulwer Lytton's *Richelieu* in preference to *A Doll's House* or Shaw's *The Man of Destiny*. Besides, Irving wasted the talents of his leading lady, Ellen Terry, the object of Shaw's admiration and recipient of his most delightful letters.

Irving was one side of the coin; William Poel was the other. Shaw admired his Shakespearean productions on approximations of the Renaissance stage, with few cuts and without scenery. This style, which restored the text to its just precedence, was later modified by one of Poel's actors, Harley Granville Barker, who produced both Shakespeare and Shaw. Two other Shakespearean actors were admired by Shaw. A teenager in Dublin, he first saw Barry Sullivan; at 92, Shaw still remembered his majesty and power. The Shakespearean acting of Forbes Robertson was so good that Shaw wrote *Caesar and Cleopatra* for him.

To study stage history is tantalizing and frustrating. As the Durgin-Park menu in Boston says, "Established Before You Were Born." Since I did not see the performances, I am prevented from reviewing them myself. A Shaw review, however brilliantly written, might impress me as sheer tosh if I had been in the audience. To get some sense of the performance, I look at photographs, drawings, and theater programs. Phonograph records from this period are rare, and the actors' voices are not always as Shaw describes them. But knowledge of the theater today is useful, since Shaw is the herald and publicizer of modern Shakespearean production, originated by Poel and Barker. Still, there *is* a veil over the Shakespearean productions that Shaw reviewed in the nineties. Under such circumstances, the frustrated theater reviewer must be resigned. Shaw is the prime evidence that Irving failed as Lear or that Ellen Terry succeeded as Imogen.

Shaw's criticism tells more about himself than about Shakespeare (chapter 6, "The Exposer Exposed"). Does Shaw apply his principles? Is he an original thinker or a word-musician after all? Shaw's criticism should be valued, not as a balanced view of the theater of the past, but as an energetic advertisement for the theater of the present. With playwrights like Ibsen and Shaw, who can deny that such advertising is justified? Although Shaw's blasts at Shakespeare the nonthinker are highly disrespectful, the blasts at Irving and his lacerated acting versions show considerable respect for Shakespeare. Despite all his bluster, Shaw is a Shakespearean fan (though certainly not a devout one). Let Shakespeare be performed whole, not dismembered. Keep Shakespeare on the stage—but find room for Ibsen and Shaw.

2

Putting Shakespeare to Use

Shaw knew all too well that Shakespeare was the hardest of acts to follow. Shakespeare was both the subject of Shaw's reviews and his competitor for the stage. Such circumstances do not make for objective criticism. In his essays, plays, and novels, Shaw made use of his rival. *King Lear* supports a point about socialist economics; a Falstaff statue is erected to remind some extremely long-lived persons of the future about the virtues of cowardice; Shakespeare is a character in Shaw's plays, once as a shameless pilferer of his contemporaries' blank verse and later, in a puppet show, as antagonist of one Shav. To write like this, Shaw needed one part ingenuity and two parts audacity. He had a plentiful supply of both.

In the preface to his first novel, *Immaturity*, Shaw claims descent from Macduff: "It was as good as being descended from Shakespear, whom I had been unconsciously resolved to reincarnate from my cradle."[1] He repeated this Shakespearean family tree on several occasions:

> I had better explain that my family traces its descent from one Shaigh, the third son of Macduff, immortalized by Shakespear as having been "from his mother's womb untimely ripped."[2]

In his admirable biography of Shaw, Hesketh Pearson is skeptical: "It occurred to me that he might not have been equally pleased if his ancestor had been, say, the Drunken Porter in the same play."[3] As soon as Shaw emerged from the cradle, he wasted no time in reading Shakespeare. By the time he left Dublin for London in 1876, he knew "everybody in Shakespear, from Hamlet to Abhorson," better than his living contemporaries.[4]

Shaw found striking resemblances between his personal life and Shakespeare's. He traces the background of Shakespeare's father, John, who failed commercially and could not give his son a university education. Shaw claims, "These circumstances interest me because they are just like my own."[5] He puts it more bluntly in the preface to *Misalliance:* "In short, I am, as to classical education, another Shakespear."[6] Shaw refused to do anything for the Bard that he would not do for himself: "I have long ceased to celebrate my own birthday; and I do not see why I should celebrate Shakespear's."[7] However, over fifty years later, Shaw admitted that he had done his share of celebrating. He had attended "bardic festivals" at Stratford-on-Avon so often that he had "come to regard it almost as a supplementary birthplace of my own."[8]

John Shakespeare and George Carr Shaw may have thrust sons into similar economic backgrounds, but there the resemblance ends. In terms of income, Shaw and Shakespeare were in different brackets:

> I am not supposed to be an exceptionally modest man; but I did not advance the fact that I have made more money by a single play than Shakespear did by all his plays put together as a simple proof that I am enormously superior to Shakespear as a playwright.[9]

But he advances the fact anyway, and the reader of *Essays in Fabian Socialism* is left to draw his own conclusions. Shakespeare did not have movie rights and overseas performances to increase his income, but on the other hand he did not have excessive taxes to whittle it away. By Renaissance standards, Shakespeare may have been better off than Shaw supposes.

Shaw moved from the economic facts of Shakespeare's life to the economic messages in his plays. A lesson is to be learned from *Hamlet,* as Shaw points out in "The Dream of Distribution According to Merit" (from the preface to *Androcles and the Lion*) : "The Sunday School idea, with its principle 'to each the income he deserves,' is really too silly for discussion. Hamlet disposed of it three hundred years ago. 'Use every man after his deserts, and who shall 'scape whipping?' "[10] In *The Intelligent Woman's Guide to Socialism and Capitalism, King Lear* provides evidence in an argument about economic self-sufficiency:

> In Shakespear's famous play, King Lear and his daughters have an argument about this. His idea of enough is having a hundred knights to wait on him. His eldest daughter thinks that fifty would be enough. Her sister does not see what he wants with any knights at all when her servants can do all he needs for him. Lear retorts that if she cuts life down to what cannot be done without, she had better throw away her fine clothes, as she would be warmer in a blanket. And to this she has no answer. Nobody can say what is enough. What is enough for a gipsy is not enough for a lady; and what is enough for one lady leaves another very discontented.[11]

"O reason not the economics!"

The Renaissance socialist (for one scene anyway) is remarkable; even more so is the funerary Shakespeare. Shaw was asked to deliver the oration for his sister Lucy, who had stopped eating, the doctor said, because she was afraid of World War I artillery fire:

> Not knowing her circle of friends I did not invite anyone to her cremation at Golders Green; but when I got there I found the chapel crowded with her adorers. In her will she had expressly forbidden any religious service; but with all those people there I felt that I could not have her thrown on the fire like a scuttle of coals; so I delivered a funeral oration, and finished by reciting the dirge from Cymbeline because
>
> Fear no more the lightning-flash,
> Nor the all-dreaded thunder-stone
>
> so nearly fitted what the doctor told me.[12]

It is surprising that Shaw did not quote his admired Bunyan. But since Shaw did not care much about his sister, perhaps he thought that Shakespeare, the second-best, would do.

This chilling description is matched by a postcard about Mrs. Shaw's last days. It was Shaw's final correspondence with Harley Granville Barker:

> Charlotte died last Sunday, the 12th. September, at half past two in the morning. She had not forgotten you.
>
> Since 1939 she has suffered much pain and lately some distress from hallucinations of crowds of people in her room; and the disease, a horror called osteitis deformans which bent and furrowed her into a Macbeth witch (an amiable one), was progressing steadily and incurably. But last Friday a miracle occurred. She suddenly threw off her years, her visions, her furrows, her distresses, and had thirty hours of youth and happiness before the little breath *she* could draw failed. By morning she looked twenty years younger than you or I ever knew her.
>
> It was a blessedly happy ending; but you could not have believed that I should be as deeply moved. You will not, I know, mind my writing this to you. She was 86. I am 87. G.B.S.[13]

The "Macbeth witch" throws this out of kilter. Shaw remembered Shakespeare once too often.

Shaw was a little more successful in relating Shakespeare to love. Shaw spent a lifetime trying to excel Shakespeare the dramatist, but there is only one recorded instance of a Shavian sonnet, addressed to Mrs. Patrick Campbell:

SHAKESPEAR SONNET

Oh wherefore in my heart that was so hard
Hast thou these tender places made to come?
Dost thou not know how I must stand on guard?
How I must keep that voice of nature dumb
That bids me to a tranquil fireside turn
And thou there with our child upon thy knees,
And makes this springtime hurt me like a burn
Because we cannot play beneath the trees?

> If I give way to thee, am I not lost,
> Divided, doubled, thrown quite off my track?
> If I forego thee, can I bear the cost
> Of craving every hour to have thee back?
>   Oh dearest Danger, I must love thee less
>   Or plunge into a devil of a mess.[14]

Criticism of this is unnecessary; the last line does the trick.

Evidently Shaw did not hesitate to relate Shakespeare to his own life, to important matters like birth, love, death of relatives, and personal income, but most of the comments about Shakespeare were geared not to Shaw's biography but to his ego. Shaw made use of Shakespeare in his plays; he also had fun at the Bard's expense in two non-dramatic pieces, "The Theatre of the Future" and "Macbeth. A Novel." The first is a short story in which Shaw projects certain changes in stage practice. The initial efforts of this theater are the three parts of *Henry VI*, "which opened the theatre to Shakespear and inaugurated the Elizabethan stage (not Mr William Poel's but an earlier XVI–XVII Century enterprise known by the same name)."[15] Contrary to late-Victorian practice, the plays were not radically revised except for one small matter:

> Mr Algernon Swinburne, however, whose all but idolatrous veneration for the Bard is well known, has undertaken to rewrite the Joan of Arc scenes from the point of view, not only of what Shakespear undoubtedly ought to have written, but of the *entente cordiale* between this country and France.[16]

Despite the best intentions, the production at The Theatre of the Future did not go quite as planned, for the management saw fit to announce:

> The Manager greatly regrets that the conclusion of the Second Part of King Henry VI was last night reduced to absurdity by the inartistic behavior of the Lancastrian army, which in the excitement of the moment defeated the Yorkists instead of retreating in confusion. In future the numbers of the contend-

ing forces will be so apportioned as to make a recurrence of this regrettable incident impossible.[17]

"Macbeth. A Novel" is a parody both of Shakespeare and of Arnold Bennett, who claimed that it is easier to write a play than a novel. Shaw could not let that pass. He ends with prose "by Arnold Bennett, John Galsworthy, or Anybody":

> They laid Macbeth in God's quiet acre in the little churchyard of Dunsinane. Malcolm erected a stately tomb there, for the credit of the institution of kingship; and the epitaph, all things considered, was not unhandsome. There was no reproach in it, no vain bitterness. It said that Macbeth had "succeeded Duncan."
> The birds are still singing on Dunsinane. The wood pigeon still coos about the coos; and Malcolm takes them frankly and generously. It is not for us to judge him, or to judge Macbeth. Macbeth was born before his time. Men call him a villain; but had the press existed in his day, a very trifling pecuniary sacrifice on his part would have made a hero of him. And, to do him justice, he was never stingy.
> Well! Well![18]

Shaw concludes, "Decidedly, when my faculties decay a little further, I shall go back to novel writing. And Arnold Bennett can fall back on writing plays."

In his plays, Shaw often falls back on Shakespeare. In *You Never Can Tell* (1896), the irrepressible waiter is named William, because (to a young customer anyway) he resembles the bust of Shakespeare in Stratford Church. Shakespeare was born in Cork, according to the mother in *O'Flaherty V.C.* (1915); Shaw describes her as a "Volumnia of the potato patch."[19] Sempronius in *The Apple Cart* (1929) has a father who arranges coronations and detests the stage, more or less:

> My father might have made millions in the theatres and film studios. But he refused to touch them because the things they

represented hadnt really happened. He didnt mind doing the
christening of Queen Elizabeth in Shakespear's Henry the
Eighth because that had really happened. It was a celebration
of royalty. But not anything romantic; not though they offered
him thousands.[20]

In *Geneva* (1938), Franco is thinly disguised as General
Flanco de Fortinbras. Mrs. Basham, Isaac Newton's house-
keeper, *"In Good King Charles's Golden Days"* (1939), is
shocked by Restoration acting: "Mr Shakespear would have
died of shame to see a woman on the stage."[21] Nell Gwynn
scoffs: "What! That author the old actors used to talk
about."[22]

In *The Doctor's Dilemma* (1906), after Dubedat's death,
B.B. (Sir Ralph Bloomfield Bonington) pronounces the
benediction, curiously:

> I think it is Shakespear who says that the good that most
> men do lives after them: the evil lies interréd with their
> bones. Yes: interréd with their bones. Believe me, Paddy, we
> are all mortal. It is the common lot, Ridgeon. Say what you
> will, Walpole, Nature's debt must be paid. If tis not to-day,
> twill be tomorrow.
>
>> To-morrow and to-morrow and to-morrow
>> After life's fitful fever they sleep well
>> And like this insubstantial bourne from which
>> No traveller returns
>> Leave not a wrack behind.
>
> *Walpole is about to speak, but B.B., suddenly and vehemently
> proceeding, extinguishes him.*
>> Out, out, brief candle:
> For nothing canst thou to damnation add;
> The readiness is all.[23]

That is a performance to rival the Duke and Dauphin's "Royal
Nonesuch." The corpse of Dubedat is proof that B.B. is
as careless with his patients as with his Shakespeare.

Shaw's most impressionable heroine, for one act, is Ellie

Dunn in *Heartbreak House* (1919). Her father says that she has remarkable strength of character because she knows Shakespeare. But Ellie is gullible; witness her reading of *Othello*. Like Desdemona, she believes the Moor's tales. Hesione Hushabye tries to disillusion her, not knowing that her husband, Hector, has done some fabling himself:

> ELLIE [*naïvely*]. Do you never read Shakespear, Hesione? That seems to me so extraordinary. I like Othello.
> MRS HUSHABYE. Do you indeed? He was jealous, wasnt he?
> ELLIE. Oh, not that. I think all the part about jealousy is horrible. But dont you think it must have been a wonderful experience for Desdemona, brought up so quietly at home, to meet a man who had been out in the world doing all sorts of brave things and having terrible adventures, and yet finding something in her that made him love to sit and talk with her and tell her about them? . . .
> MRS HUSHABYE. Ellie darling: have you noticed that some of those stories that Othello told Desdemona couldnt have happened?
> ELLIE. Oh no. Shakespear thought they could have happened.
> MRS HUSHABYE. Hm! Desdemona thought they could have happened. But they didnt.
> ELLIE. Why do you look so enigmatic about it? You are such a sphinx: I never know what you mean.
> MRS HUSHABYE. Desdemona would have found him out if she had lived, you know. I wonder was that why he strangled her!
> ELLIE. Othello was not telling lies.
> MRS HUSHABYE. How do you know?
> ELLIE. Shakespear would have said if he was.[24]

When Ellie-Desdemona finds out Hector-Othello, she grows older and wiser very fast. She is so disillusioned that she says, "There seems to be nothing real in the world except my father and Shakespear."[25]

The echoes from Shakespeare enliven Shaw's worst play, *Back to Methuselah* (1920). In Part II, an enthusiast for biology rhapsodizes about "The cloud-capped towers, the solemn binnacles, the gorgeous temples, the great globe it-

self: yea, all that it inherit shall dissolve, and, like this influential pageant faded, leave not a rack behind." He insists:
"That's biology, you know: good sound biology."[26] In Part
IV, Zoo, one of the long-lived people, talks about the statue
of a local hero:

> All I can tell you about it is that a thousand years ago, when
> the whole world was given over to you short-lived people, there
> was a war called the War to end War. In the war which
> followed it about ten years later, hardly any soldiers were
> killed; but seven of the capital cities of Europe were wiped
> out of existence. It seems to have been a great joke; for the
> statesmen who thought they had sent ten million common
> men to their deaths were themselves blown into fragments
> with their houses and families, while the ten million men lay
> snugly in the caves they had dug for themselves. Later on
> even the houses escaped: but their inhabitants were poisoned
> by gas that spared no living soul. Of course the soldiers starved
> and ran wild; and that was the end of pseudo-Christian civiliza-
> tion. The last civilized thing that happened was that the states-
> men discovered that cowardice was a great patriotic virtue;
> and a public monument was erected to its first preacher, an
> ancient and very fat sage called Sir John Falstaff. Well [point-
> ing], thats Falstaff.[27]

Falstaff's author is a character in two one-act plays by
Shaw. *The Dark Lady of the Sonnets* (1910) is an appeal
for a National Theatre to celebrate the tercentenary of
Shakespeare's death. The preface consists of speculations
about Frank Harris's speculations about Shakespeare's personal life. Like most commentators on Shakespearean biography, Shaw flounders in a vacuum. The play is another
matter, an amusing Shavian shrug. The cast of characters includes Queen Elizabeth (who enters sleepwalking and ex-
claiming that "all the perfumes of Arabia will not whiten
this Tudor hand"), the Dark Lady, and "Shakespear." This
fellow specializes in stealing pithy remarks. The beefeater
at Buckingham Palace says, "There, indeed, you many say
of frailty that its name is woman."[28] The poet, observing

that many of the beefeater's degree have music in their soul, promptly writes, "Frailty: thy name is woman!" The beef-eater asks him if he is a snapper-up of such unconsidered trifles. "Oh! Immortal phrase!" sighs the poet, as he writes it down. Upon entering, the Dark Lady cuffs the Queen and sends Shakespear sprawling:

> THE CLOAKED LADY [*in towering wrath, throwing off her cloak and turning in outraged majesty on her assailant*] High treason.
> THE DARK LADY [*recognizing her and falling on her knees in abject terror*] Will: I am lost: I have struck the Queen.
> THE MAN [*sitting up as majestically as his ignominious posture allows*] Woman: you have struck WILLIAM SHAKE-SPEAR!!!!!![29]

After the Queen dismisses the Dark Lady, Shakespear gets down to business, asking the Queen to endow a National Theatre. The Queen must refuse:

> I dare not offend my unruly Puritans by making so lewd a place as the playhouse a public charge; and there be a thousand things to be done in this London of mine before your poetry can have its penny from the general purse. I tell thee, Master Will, it will be three hundred years and more before my subjects learn that man cannot live by bread alone, but by every word that cometh from the mouth of those whom God inspires.[30]

Elizabeth and Shakespear go their separate ways. For Shaw, the lewd playhouse is not merely a place of amusement, any more than the National Gallery or the British Museum, although "these institutions are commercial failures, just as Westminster Abbey is a commercial failure."[31]

A short, unhappy story can serve as a sequel. The plea for a National Theatre fell on almost deaf ears:

> After some years of effort the result was a single handsome subscription from a German gentleman. Like the celebrated swearer in the anecdote when the cart containing all his

household goods lost its tailboard at the top of the hill and let its contents roll in ruin to the bottom, I can only say, "I cannot do justice to this situation," and let it pass without another word.[32]

But justice has been done. On October 22, 1963, the National Theatre opened with *Hamlet*. It has presented a number of playwrights, including both Shakespeare and Shaw.[33]

Shakespeare is a character again in the puppet play, *Shakes Versus Shav* (1949), written by Shaw at 93. This tomfoolery involves a fight, verbal and physical; Shav flattens Shakes with a right to the chin. Shakes points with pride to Macbeth; Shav replies, "He has been bettered/By Walter Scott's Rob Roy. Behold, and blush."[34] They appear, and Rob Roy slices off Macbeth's head. Undaunted, Shakes demands, "Where is thy Hamlet? Couldst thou write King Lear?" Shav replies, "Aye, with his daughters all complete. Couldst thou/Have written Heartbreak House? Behold my Lear."[35] Then according to the stage direction, "A transparency is suddenly lit up, showing Captain Shotover seated, as in Millais' picture called North-West Passage, with a young woman of virginal beauty." The poets spar again and the play ends with Shakes having the last word:

> SHAV.   Peace, jealous Bard:
> We both are mortal. For a moment suffer
> My glimmering light to shine.
>   *A light appears between them.*
> SHAKES. Out, out, brief candle! [*He puffs it out.*]
>   *Darkness. The play ends.*[36]

In the preface to *The Dark Lady of the Sonnets*, Shaw says: "if I had been born in 1556 instead of in 1856, I should have taken to blank verse and given Shakespear a harder run for his money than all the other Elizabethans put together."[37] In fact, Shaw had written a play in the Elizabethan style, *The Admirable Bashville* (1901), a reworking of his novel, *Cashel Byron's Profession*. Cashel loves a lady of breeding, and in her society his profession of boxing is only slightly less opprobrious than Mrs. Warren's. He wins the lady, none the less.

Shaw insisted that writing the play was no problem whatever:

> It may be asked why I wrote The Admirable Bashville in blank verse. My answer is that the operation of the copyright law of that time (now happily superseded) left only a week to write it in. Blank verse is so childishly easy and expeditious (hence, by the way, Shakespear's copious output) that by adopting it I was enabled to do within the week what would have cost me a month in prose.[38]

In the play, Victorian characters mouth the speech of three hundred years before. The verse sounds remotely like the genuine Renaissance article, for example, when the heroine, Lydia Carew, rhapsodizes:

> Lo, the leaves
> That hide my drooping boughs! Mock me—poor maid!—
> Deride with joyous comfortable chatter
> These stolen feathers. Laugh at me, the clothed one.
> Laugh at the mind fed on foul air and books.
> Books! Art! And Culture! Oh, I shall go mad.
> Give me a mate that never heard of these,
> A sylvan god, tree born in heart and sap;
> Or else, eternal maidhood be my hap.[39]

Shaw writes several varieties of speech, from Lydia's arboreal plaint to the Ercles' vein of Bashville, Lydia's servant:

> Gods! how she hangs on's arm! I am alone.
> Now let me lift the cover from my soul.
> O wasted humbleness! Deluded diffidence!
> How often have I said, Lie down, poor footman:
> She'll never stoop to thee, rear as thou wilt
> Thy powder to the sky. And now, by Heaven,
> She stoops below me; condescends upon
> This hero of the pothouse, whose exploits,

> Writ in my character from my last place,
> Would damn me into ostlerdom. And yet
> Theres an eternal justice in it; for
> By so much as the ne'er subduéd Indian
> Excels the servile negro, doth this ruffian
> Precedence take of me. *"Ich dien."* Damnation!
> I serve. My motto should have been, "I scalp."[40]

Bashville resorts to something less assertive: professional boxing. He does not marry Lydia, however. She tells him about her prior attachment with Cashel, and as long as "polyandry/ Rests foreign to the British social scheme,/ Your love is hopeless."[41]

It was a short step from writing a play in mock-Shakespearean to rewriting a play (or at least part of it) by Shakespeare. Shaw had a long running battle with *Cymbeline,* the most famous engagement taking place in *The Saturday Review* as "Blaming the Bard" (1896). In 1937, he revised the last act. In the foreword to *Cymbeline Refinished,* Shaw justifies this:

> And now consider the practice of Shakespear himself. Tolstoy declared that the original Lear is superior to Shakespear's rehandling, which he abhorred as immoral. Nobody has ever agreed with him. Will it be contended that Shakespear had no right to refashion Hamlet? If he had spoiled both plays, that would be a reason for reviving them without Shakespear's transfigurations, but not for challenging Shakespear's right to make them.[42]

The reasoning is impeccable, and the results are lively enough to warrant the effort. Shaw maintains that he had no difficulty in rewriting:

> In doing so I had to follow the Shakespearean verse pattern to match the 89 lines of Shakespear's text which I retained. This came very easily to me. It happened when I was a child that one of the books I delighted in was an illustrated Shakespear, with a picture and two or three lines of text underneath it on every third or fourth page. Ever since, Shake-

spearean blank verse has been to me as natural a form of literary expression as the Augustan English to which I was brought up in Dublin, or the latest London fashion in dialogue.[43]

Shaw pruned much of the act. Shakespeare's Act V has over 800 lines, Shaw's 300. Shakespeare includes battles between Romans and Britons, a prison masque in which Jupiter appears to the sleeping hero, Posthumus, and a final scene whereby the heroine and hero are reconciled and a truce with the Romans is made by Cymbeline, the British King. Shaw cuts the battle scenes, which he terms "ludicrous," and the masque, which he rather likes. But the masque did not fit in with his purpose: "to rewrite the act as Shakespear might have written it if he had been post-Ibsen and post-Shaw instead of post-Marlowe."

In an introductory scene by Shaw, the battle is described. Then follows Shakespeare's first scene; Posthumus regrets that he has given the order for the death of Imogen, his wife. From here on, Shaw takes over. Posthumus meets the villain, Iachimo, who has falsely maligned Imogen. When they recognize each other, they waste no time in drawing swords:

> POSTHUMUS. This only: I have had her murdered, I.
> And at my best am worser than her worst.
> IACHIMO. We are damned for this. [*on guard*] Let's cut each other's throats.
> POSTHUMUS [*drawing*] Ay, let us.[44]

The Britons enter and separate the swordsmen. When Imogen and Posthumus have recognized each other, he says, "Mountains of mortal guilt/ That crushed me are now lifted from my breast." Iachimo admits his perfidy, but Imogen is not satisfied. After all, her husband wanted to have her killed. She complains, "My husband thinks that all is settled now/ And this a happy ending!" She appeals to her new friends, Guiderius and Arviragus. Immediately their real identity is disclosed. Their guardian, Belarius, had stolen them away twenty years before; they are actually sons of the King.

At this point they begin acting very modern indeed. Guiderius asks, "Can I change fathers as I'd change my shirt?" Arviragus tells Cymbeline, "Well, we have reached an age/ When fathers' helps are felt as hindrances." Belarius asks the king to pardon them; the fault is his for their up-bringing. Guiderius disagrees: "The fault, if fault there be, is in my Maker. I am of no man's making. I am I: Take me or leave me." Iachimo points out that this is the future king of England. Guiderius's reply suggests certain dynastic problems of 1936:

> I am to be, forsooth, another Cloten,
> Plagued by the chatter of his train of flatterers,
> Compelled to worship priest invented gods,
> Not free to wed the woman of my choice,
> Being stopped at every turn by some old fool
> Crying, "You must not," or, still worse, "You must."
> Oh no, sir: give me back the dear old cave
> And my unflattering four footed friends.
> I abdicate, and pass the throne to Polydore.[45]

To which his brother enthusiastically replies: "Do you, by heavens? Thank you for nothing, brother."

Although Imogen still remembers her husband's un-gracious behavior, Cymbeline cannot be bothered with such things:

> God's patience, man, take your wife home to bed.
> You're man and wife: nothing can alter that.
> Are there more plots to unravel? Each one here,
> It seems, is someone else. [*To Imogen*] Go change your dress
> For one becoming to your sex and rank.
> Have you no shame?
> IMOGEN. None.
> CYMBELINE. How? None!
> IMOGEN. All is lost.
> Shame, husband, happiness, and faith in Man.
> He is not even sorry.
> POSTHUMUS. I'm too happy.[46]

Iachimo tries to placate her, insisting that she is a very worthy lady but not quite an angel. Imogen finally decides to bear the cross of the modern woman: "I will not laugh./ I must go home and make the best of it/ As other women must." The act ends, like Shakespeare's, with a truce between Romans and Britons.

It would be hard to mistake those lines for Shakespeare. Shaw has evidently been at work. It is literature's loss (perhaps) that he did not completely rewrite any play by Shakespeare, but in a sense *Saint Joan* is a reworking of *I Henry VI*. Shaw detests Shakespeare's characterization of Joan as a witch and a whore:

> This portrait of Joan is not more authentic than the descriptions in the London papers of George Washington in 1780, of Napoleon in 1803, of the German Crown Prince in 1915, or of Lenin in 1917. It ends in mere scurrility. The impression left by it is that the playwright, having begun by an attempt to make Joan a beautiful and romantic figure, was told by his scandalized company that English patriotism would never stand a sympathetic representation of a French conqueror of English troops, and that unless he at once introduced all the old charges against Joan of being a sorceress and a harlot, and assumed her to be guilty of all of them, his play could not be produced.[47]

In a letter to Mrs. Patrick Campbell, Shaw refers to the "piffling libel in Henry VI, which reminds me that one of my scenes will be Voltaire and Shakespear running down bye streets in heaven to avoid meeting Joan."[48] This epilogue to the Epilogue of *Saint Joan* was never written.

In the preface to *Three Plays for Puritans*, which include *Caesar and Cleopatra*, Shaw wrote "Better than Shakespear?" That is, to be sure, a question. "Better than Shakespear" was a theater review; the superior writer was not Shaw but John Bunyan.[49] Shaw did not claim that he could write a more entertaining play about Caesar and Cleopatra. He did maintain that a playwright with a different moral viewpoint has the prerogative to reinterpret the past:

The writing of practicable stage plays does not present an infinite scope to human talent; and the playwrights who magnify its difficulties are humbugs. The summit of their art has been attained again and again. No man will ever write a better tragedy than Lear, a better comedy than Le Festin de Pierre or Peer Gynt, a better opera than Don Giovanni, a better music drama than The Niblung's Ring, or, for the matter of that, better fashionable plays and melodramas than are now being turned out by writers whom nobody dreams of mocking with the word immortal. It is the philosophy, the outlook on life, that changes, not the craft of the playwright.[50]

Different authors look at the same characters in different ways. Shakespeare revised Homer in *Troilus and Cressida*. "This," Shaw says, "did not in the least involve any pretence on Shakespear's part to be a greater poet than Homer."[51] Shaw, in redrawing the characters of Caesar and Cleopatra, does not pretend to be a greater playwright than Shakespeare. He has denied it in plain terms:

It was the overwhelming contrast with Ibsen that explains my Saturday Review campaign against the spurious part of Shakespear's reputation. But the notion that I ever claimed crudely that my plays, or anybody's plays, were better written than Shakespear's, is absurd.[52]

Modesty was not one of Shaw's vices, but he comes close to it here. Shaw is not all bluster and outraged virtue by any means. He had little respect for Shakespeare the philosopher, but he never underestimated the dramatic skill of his competitor. "No man will ever write a better tragedy than Lear," he says. This was his favorite Shakespearean play, but he wrote little about it. There is no complete review or essay, only infrequent remarks in praise. He talks about a question that his fellow critics failed to ask:

True, it is impossible to say what a man can do until he tries. I may before the end of this year write a tragedy on the subject of King Lear that will efface Shakespear's; but if I do it will be a surprise, not perhaps to myself, but to the public. It is certain that if I took the work in hand I should be able to turn out five acts about King Lear that would be, at least, grammatical, superficially coherent, and arranged in lines that would scan. And I doubt not at all that some friendly and ingenious critic would say of it, "Lear is, from beginning to end, a remarkable work, and one which nobody but an English author could have written. Every page bears the stamp of G.B.S.'s genius; and no higher praise can be awarded to it than to say that it is fully worthy of his reputation." What critic would need to be so unfriendly as to face the plain question, "Has the author been able for his subject?"[53]

Shaw plainly implied that he was not able for the subject. He knew enough not to bite off more than he could chew.

Goethe said that he had an advantage as a German writer; if he were English, Shakespeare would overpower him: "I should not have known what to do. I could not have gone on with such fresh light-heartedness; but should have had to bethink myself, and look about for a long time, to find some new outlet."[54] As an Irishman, Shaw was better equipped to resist Shakespeare's power. Shaw was not overwhelmed and had no difficulty in retaining his lightness of heart, about Shakespeare and things in general. As he said about *Man and Superman,* in a letter to Tolstoy (14 February 1910) :[55]

You said that my manner in that book was not serious enough—that I made people laugh in my most earnest moments. But why should I not? Why should humour and laughter be excommunicated? Suppose the world were only one of God's jokes, would you work any the less to make it a good joke instead of a bad one?

3
Shaw's Principles of Criticism

Kenneth Tynan says that most collections of theater reviews "resemble nothing so much as a bag of unstrung beads."[1] This does not apply to Shaw, who intends to revitalize the stage, both by reviewing Shakespeare and Ibsen and by writing plays. Shaw welds his reviews by a consistent (and sometimes tiresomely reiterated) point of view, what he called "a siege laid to the theatre of the XIXth century by an author who had to cut his own way into it at the point of the pen, and throw some of its defenders into the moat."[2] Shaw's wit serves this point of view. In his reviews, Shaw considers both plays and performances.

Harold Clurman argues that a performance makes sense only when it is related to the play:

> To my (partial) astonishment, I find that most discussions of Shakespeare or Shaw revivals center on our taste for this or that particular actor, for this or that particular stage arrangement—quite apart from any unified meaning the producers hoped to give their presentation. The text itself is taken for granted, as if, to begin with, we all unquestionably knew what *Hamlet* or *King Lear* or *Saint Joan* are truly about.[3]

Clurman's reviews explain and clarify both play and performance. He acknowledges the debt of theater reviewers to Shaw, who combined the philosophical and the practical, what the stage ought to be, and what it actually is (and, most often, what it is not). Shaw fervently admires or detests plays; he radiates equal warmth about the productions.

35

In criticizing Shakespeare, Shaw had a definite purpose in mind. Although professional jealousy undoubtedly played a large part, it was by no means the sole motivation. Shaw made the most convincing explanation for his behavior in reference to Ernest Newman's attack on Richard Strauss's *Elektra*. Shaw came to Strauss's defense. Newman objected that Shaw was not acting true to form. Why attack Shakespeare but defend Strauss? Shaw replied:

Now for Mr Newman's final plea, with its implicit compliment to myself, which I quite appreciate. That plea is that he did to Strauss only as I did to Shakespear. Proud as I am to be Mr Newman's exemplar, the cases are not alike. If the day should ever dawn in England on a Strauss made into an idol; on an outrageous attribution to him of omniscience and infallibility; on a universal respect for his reputation accompanied by an ignorance of his works so gross that the most grotesque mutilations and travesties of his scores will pass without protest as faithful performances of them; on essays written to shew how Clytemnestra was redeemed by her sweet womanly love for Aegisthus, and Elektra a model of filial piety to all middle-class daughters; on a generation of young musicians taught that they must copy all Strauss's progressions and rhythms and instrumentation and all the rest of it if they wish to do high-class work; in short, on all the follies of Bardolatry transferred to Strauss, then I shall give Mr Newman leave to say his worst of Strauss, were it only for Strauss's own sake. But that day has not yet dawned. The current humbug is all the other way. The geese are in full cackle to prove that Strauss is one of themselves instead of the greatest living composer. I made war on the duffers who idolized Shakespear. Mr Newman took the side of the duffers who are trying to persuade the public that Strauss is an impostor making an offensive noise with an orchestra of marrow-bones and cleavers. It is not enough to say that I scoffed, and that therefore I have no right to complain of other people scoffing. Any fool can scoff. The serious matter is which side you scoff at. Scoffing at pretentious dufferdom is a public duty; scoffing at an advancing torchbearer is a deadly sin.[4]

This letter would leave a better taste in the mouth if Shaw

had admitted that he often scoffed at an advancing torch-bearer, Brahms. In any case, Shaw's explanation for his behavior is a defense of the underdog. Shakespeare needed no partisan, but Strauss did. Strauss had not yet acquired an appreciative audience; Shakespeare had an overly appreciative audience that listened to no one else. In the spirit of fair play, Shaw tried to right the balance.

This letter suggests that Shaw's criticism of Shakespeare was determined largely by prevailing attitudes. Shakespeare was idolized; therefore, the idol had to fall. Imagine that the reverse attitude had been prevalent in the nineteenth century, that Shakespeare had been denigrated or ignored. Then Shaw might have vehemently defended him. Shaw found disinterested criticism anemic; he wanted to change people's minds, or at least set them thinking. Shaw used the cold-water treatment. This does not always have the desired effect. Cold water can jolt someone out of his point of view, or convince him that he is absolutely right in having ideas different from those exhibitionists who want change. A subtler, more insidious way of writing may be more persuasive, or so subtle that most people do not get the point. Shaw made sure that everyone got his point. Subtlety was the farthest thing from his mind. He woke up his readers, but it is hard to determine how many minds he changed.

Shaw often gives the impression that he detested Shakespeare. This is not the case at all. Shaw knew Shakespeare backwards and forwards, having read him avidly since childhood. He was "unaffectedly fond" of Shakespeare, not of actor-managers' editions and revivals but of "the plays as Shakespear wrote them, played straight through line by line and scene by scene as nearly as possible under the conditions of representation for which they were designed."[5] Eric Bentley has said that Shaw "in Shakespearean discussion resembles an atheist who in religious controversy turns out to know and relish the Bible more than the godly."[6] Shaw was not really a Shakespeare atheist. He was more the avatar of a remarkably curious but undeniably lively sect called Shavianism. This sect, it is true, militantly opposed the godhead of the Renaissance playwright. However, it was quite willing to give him his due as a human being. Not that the sect approved of the total removal of godlike figures. Witness the praise for the new Nordic deity, Ibsen.

Shaw then was both iconoclast and iconolater. Condemnation was accompanied by plans for improvement. His iconoclasm was no anarchic undermining of the artistic powers that be; it sprang from his own moral convictions. Art without moral purpose was inferior art. For instance, Shaw objected to the moral tone of the movies:

> The result is that the movie play has supplanted the old-fashioned tract and Sunday-school prize: it is reeking with morality but dares not touch virtue. And virtue, which is defiant and contemptuous of morality even when it has no practical quarrel with it, is the lifeblood of high drama.[7]

Shaw sneers at middle-class platitudes, nothing more than overblown etiquette. Virtue for Shaw is much more rigorous and demanding; it is behavior penetrated and inspired by moral purpose.

Shaw bristled that audiences persistently ignored the serious purposes of the drama. This necessitated sleight-of-hand by playwrights with a message:

> No fact is ever attended to by the average citizen until the neglect of it has killed enough of his neighbors to thoroughly frighten him. He does not believe that happiness exists except in dreams; and when by chance he dreams of his real life, he feels defrauded, as if he had been cheated into night-work by his employer or his clients. Hence the more unnatural, impossible, unreasonable, and morally fraudulent a theatrical entertainment is, the better he likes it. He abhors the play with a purpose, because it says to him, "Here, sir, is a fact which you ought to attend to." This, however, produces the happy result that the great dramatic poets, who are all incor-

rigible moralists and preachers, are forced to produce plays of
extraordinary interest in order to induce our audiences of
shirkers and dreamers to swallow the pill.[8]

The great dramatic poets are all incorrigible moralists and
preachers. One suspects that Shaw would add a corollary
to his axiom: dramatic poets (like Shakespeare) who are not
incorrigible moralists and preachers fall short of greatness.
Shaw suggests that his own plays would be straight essays
if his immature audiences would only stand for it. Far be
it from Shaw to enliven the play and display his craft. He
does not consider the possibility that the audiences may not
take their medicine, that they could suck off the sugar coat-
ing and spit out the pill. For Shaw, plays with a purpose
were essential, but he also had an extraordinary knack for
dialogue and characterization. Sometimes Shaw's purpose
is blunted and overwhelmed by his own talents. Then he
is not such an incorrigible moralist and preacher. He is
more of an incorrigible entertainer. By Shaw's own standards,
this would make him less than a great playwright. Some
people, though, do not link great playwrights with a pulpit.
They would find Shaw the entertainer a finer fellow than
Shaw the moralizer.

In the preface to *Three Plays for Puritans,* Shaw explains
his attitude about art of high purpose. This Puritan will not
repeat Shakespeare's error of making "sexual infatuation a
tragic theme." Shaw's Cleopatra is no Circe, his Caesar no
hog.[9] He recoils against art that glorifies and deifies sexual
love:

I have, I think, always been a Puritan in my attitude towards
Art. I am as fond of fine music and handsome building as
Milton was, or Cromwell, or Bunyan; but if I found that
they were becoming the instruments of a systematic idolatry
of sensuousness, I would hold it good statesmanship to blow
every cathedral in the world to pieces with dynamite, organ
and all, without the least heed to the screams of the art
critics and cultured voluptuaries. And when I see that the

nineteenth century has crowned the idolatry of Art with the deification of Love, so that every poet is supposed to have pierced to the holy of holies when he has announced that Love is the Supreme, or the Enough, or the All, I feel that Art was safer in the hands of the most fanatical of Cromwell's major generals than it will be if ever it gets into mine. The pleasures of the senses I can sympathize with and share; but the substitution of sensuous ectasy for intellectual activity and honesty is the very devil.[10]

That must be taken with a grain of salt (at least). Shaw was more of the aesthete than he liked to admit. For instance, his interest in music is often divorced from moral considerations. Shaw is caught up by it and does not bother to relate it to "intellectual activity and honesty." When he does make that kind of connection, as in *The Perfect Wagnerite* (a socialist's view of the *Ring*), he veers toward silliness, for example, in describing Alberic's cave: "This glowing place need not be a mine: it might just as well be a match-factory, with yellow phosphorus, phossy jaw, a large dividend, and plenty of clergymen shareholders."[11] *The Perfect Wagnerite* was written in 1898, two years before the preface to *Three Plays for Puritans*. The Puritan regrets that the *Ring* finishes with a "lapse into panacea-mongering didacticism by the holding up of Love as the remedy for all evils and the solvent of all social difficulties."[12] Brünnhilde's immolation scene is "psychologically identical with the scene of Cleopatra and the dead Antony in Shakespear's tragedy."[13]

Shaw is a fine music reviewer, because he can project his own sensuous appreciation. He first makes and then rejects the pilgrimage to Sybaris. Shaw feels compelled to play the dutiful servant of virtue and the higher intellectual spheres, even when he is in fact paying homage to the sensuous. What Shaw was and what Shaw professed to be were not necessarily the same. In this review, he does not sound like an organ dynamiter:

In the ardent regions where all the rest are excited and

vehement, Mozart alone is completely self-possessed: where they are clutching their bars with a grip of iron and forging them with Cyclopean blows, his gentleness of touch never deserts him: he is considerate, economical, practical under the same pressure of inspiration that throws your Titan into convulsions. This is the secret of his unpopularity with Titan fanciers. We all in our native barbarism have a relish for the strenuous: your tenor whose B flat is like the bursting of a boiler always brings down the house, even when the note brutally effaces the song. . . . With Mozart you are safe from inebriety. Hurry, excitement, eagerness, loss of consideration, are to him purely comic or vicious states of mind: he gives us Monostatos and the Queen of Night on the stage, but not in his chamber music. Now it happens that I have, deep in my nature, which is quite as deep as the average rainfall in England, a frightful contempt for your Queens of Night and Titans and their like. The true Parnassian air acts on these people like oxygen on a mouse: it first excites them, and then kills them. Give me the artist who breathes it like a native, and goes about his work in it as quietly as a common man goes about his ordinary business. Mozart did so; and that is why I like him.[14]

Shaw hit on what is distinctive in Mozart. He did not deny that he was fond of music, as this review proves. But he did object to idolatry. Instead of prostrating himself before Mozart, he simply heard what was there, and liked it, enormously. A listener like that must have an inkling of sensuous ecstasy.

Mozart's Don Giovanni is a libertine; Shaw's Don Juan is a Puritan representing intellectual activity and honesty, while the Devil represents sensuous ecstasy (Man and Superman, Act III). Although Shaw weights the scales in favor of Don Juan, the Devil could not be more appealing. The argument is not one-sided by any means.

Shaw the potential dynamiter of cathedrals resembles the berater of Shakespeare. When a "systematic idolatry of sensuousness" developed, Shaw's Puritan hackles rose. He took as much pleasure from Shakespeare as "cultured voluptuaries" did, but pleasure was not sufficient. Shaw demanded more, and Shakespeare, he thought, was not giving it to him. Shaw tried to fulfill the need for "intellectual activity and honesty," in short, the need for Ibsen. Shaw's campaign for Ibsen can be traced back to his Puritan ideas about art. *Our Theatres in the Nineties* could be subtitled "Three Volumes of Reviews for Puritans."

Shaw, as advocate of the Higher Puritanism, had no time for the lower variety, as practiced by the official guardians of theatrical morality. The censorship of plays can be traced back to 1544, when Henry VIII appointed a Master of Plays, Revels, and Masques. The censor's hand grew heavy in 1737, during Robert Walpole's administration; Henry Fielding had to stop writing anti-government plays and start writing novels, thus providing the only good argument in four hundred years for censorship. Shaw ran into difficulty with the Lord Chamberlain and his reader of plays. The censorial thumbs went down for *Mrs Warren's Profession* (1894), *The Shewing-Up of Blanco Posnet* (1909), and *Press Cuttings* (1909). The ban on *Press Cuttings* was soon lifted, but the other two plays did not receive public productions in London until 1926 and 1920.

Shaw, making no attempt to flatter the Lord Chamberlain, argued that censorship would have been disastrous for Shakespeare. If he had been a modern playwright, the Lord Chamberlain might have vetoed him too. In Gilbert and Sullivan's *Utopia Limited,* the South Sea island is reorganized on British lines. A judge of the Utopian Supreme Court comments on what had happened to the stage: "Are you aware that the Lord Chamberlain, who has his own views as to the best means of elevating the national drama, has declined to license any play that is not in blank verse and three hundred years old—as in England?"[15]

Shaw's finest writing on censorship is the preface to *The Shewing-Up of Blanco Posnet.* (The play is not nearly so good.) Shaw argues that censorship is a sign of national

ill health: "The nation's morals are like its teeth: the more
decayed they are the more it hurts to touch them."[16] He
doubts again that *Hamlet* would have passed the censor:

> He refuses to license Ghosts exactly as he would refuse to
> license Hamlet if it were submitted to him as a new play. He
> would license even Hamlet if certain alterations were made
> in it. He would disallow the incestuous relationship between
> the King and Queen. He would probably insist on the substi-
> tution of some fictitious country for Denmark in deference to
> the near relations of our reigning house with that realm. He
> would certainly make it an absolute condition that the closet
> scene, in which a son, in an agony of shame and revulsion, re-
> proaches his mother for her relations with his uncle, should be
> struck out as unbearably horrifying and improper.[17]

Shaw advocates no half-way solution to the problem of
censorship; the best thing is to get rid of it: "As the tradition which makes Malvolio not only Master of the Revels
but master of the Mind of England, and which has come
down to us from Henry VIII, is manifestly doomed to the
dustbin, the sooner it goes there the better."[18] The House
of Commons has now ended the Lord Chamberlain's power
to censor. On September 25, 1968, Malvolio bowed out.

For Shaw, it was axiomatic that art should have moral
purpose (but certainly not as defined by the Lord Chamberlain), that drama should relate to life. In the preface to
Overruled, he talks about holding the mirror up to nature:

> Theatrical art begins as the holding up to Nature of a dis-
> torting mirror. In this phase it pleases people who are childish
> enough to believe that they can see what they look like and
> what they are when they look at a true mirror. Naturally they
> think that a true mirror can teach them nothing. Only by
> giving them back some monstrous image can the mirror amuse
> or terrify them. It is not until they grow up to the point at
> which they learn that they know very little about themselves,
> and that they do not see themselves in a true mirror as other
> people see them, that they become consumed with curiosity
> as to what they really are like, and begin to demand that

the stage shall be a mirror of such accuracy and intensity of
illumination that they shall be able to get glimpses of their
real selves in it, and also learn a little how they appear to
other people.[19]

Shaw is arguing for a theater that shows things as they are.
The theater that holds the mirror up to nature is the theater
of Ibsen and Shaw. Considerable confidence is expressed
here in the tastes of audiences. They will, Shaw assumes,
eventually turn away from pap and feed on more substantial
fare. Shaw wrote this in 1912, when he had finally become
a box-office success. In the nineties, Shaw would have flayed
audiences and told them what their tastes should be. Thus
does a successful box office change the most restive of men.

Shaw did not always favor the idea of art as mirror. In
"The Author's Apology" to *Mrs Warren's Profession*, Shaw
had said that "drama is no mere setting up of the camera
to nature: it is the presentation in parable of the conflict
between Man's will and his environment: in a word, of
problem."[20] As Martin Meisel points out, Shaw made a
similar point over forty years later, in 1948:

Holding a mirror up to nature is not a correct definition of
a playwright's art. A mirror reflects what is before it. Hold
it up to any street at noonday and it shews a crowd of people
and vehicles and tells you nothing about them. . . . Shakespear's mirror was for the actor, to teach not to saw the air
and look like nothing on earth. The playwright has more to
do than to watch and wave: the policeman does that much;
but the playwright must interpret the passing show by parables.[21]

It is remarkable that Shaw's idea changed so little, since
his plays in each period are completely different. The old
Shaw entitled his plays "fables." The parables of the young
Shaw were much more down-to-earth (and much more
coherent). In the preface to *Overruled*, Shaw had said that
a play should reflect life. But he is not consistent; he also

said that interpretation is the important thing. How many, I wonder, have found Shaw's plays "a mirror of such accuracy and intensity of illumination that they shall be able to get glimpses of their real selves in it?" Few people are blessed with the wit and vivacity of Shaw's characters. If Shaw's mirror reflected accurately, the characters would be much less exuberant and appealing.

Shaw's plays, like parables, are devices for teaching and preaching. Shaw thought that audiences should be amused as well as enlightened. As an expert public speaker, he knew how to get an audience in the palm of his hand. The theater was also a platform, but different techniques had to be used. The public speaker could move directly to his points and use all his forensic powers to persuade. The playwright was compelled to use more devious means, to ornament his points by a story. A theater audience that enjoyed itself was more vulnerable to persuasion. Shaw thought of his plays as flanking movements, his essays as frontal attacks.

Shaw talked again about the playwright as interpreter of life (without parables this time) in the preface to *Three Plays by Brieux:*

> But the great dramatist has something better to do than to amuse either himself or his audience. He has to interpret life. This sounds a mere pious phrase of literary criticism; but a moment's consideration will discover its meaning and its exactitude. Life as it appears to us in our daily experience is an unintelligible chaos of happenings. You pass Othello in the bazaar in Aleppo, Iago on the jetty in Cyprus, and Desdemona in the nave of St. Mark's in Venice without the slightest clue to their relations to one another.[22]

Shaw sometimes sounds like Arnold. Here he talks about an interpretation of life, and "criticisms of life" are mentioned in his first review of Shakespeare for *The Saturday Review.* Such pious phrases do not quite sum up what Shaw had in mind. Not only does a great dramatist interpret life; he also animates and heightens it. Shaw did not really admire an author whose creations were not more vivid than real people.

In the preface to *Farfetched Fables,* Shaw talks about mental-association tests. The objects and names would remind him of literary characters, not real people: "Deeply as I was interested in politics, Hamlet and Falstaff are more alive to me than any living politician or even any relative."[23] Shaw would not have gone so far as Oscar Wilde, who said that life imitates art; but he did feel that in certain respects art could improve on life, giving it shape, vitality, and point. Shaw concludes his argument in the preface by trying to answer the question he had raised, "Am I A Pathological Case?":

> All I can plead is that as events as they actually occur mean no more than a passing crowd to a policeman on point duty, they must be arranged in some comprehensible order as stories. Without this there can be no history, no morality, no social conscience. Thus the historian, the story teller, the playwright and his actors, the poet, the mathematician, and the philosopher, are functionaries without whom civilization would not be possible. I conclude that I was born a story teller because one was needed. I am therefore not a disease but a social necessity.[24]

And so he is. The remarkable thing is that here he counts himself a social necessity not primarily as philosopher, gadfly, or propagandist, but as storyteller.

Shaw maintained that as critic and playwright he was valuable chiefly as persuader and cleanser of men's minds. Art, clearly subservient to propaganda, is a means of improving men, morals, and society. An article by Dixon Scott suggested that Shaw's propaganda was not so important as his art. Shaw found this a ridiculous instance of putting the cart before the horse:

> But I was finally shocked by his preposterous reversal of the natural relative importance of manner and matter. He quoted

a long sentence of mine, which derived a certain cumulative
intensity from the fact that it was an indictment of civilization, as a specimen of style, and then, with an amazingly
callous indifference to the fact that he, like the rest of us,
was guilty on all its counts, simply asked, with eager curiosity,
and a joyous sense of being the very man to answer the question, "Now what pose is this?" It was very much as if I had
told him the house was on fire, and he had said, "How admirably monosyllabic!" and left the nursery stairs burning
unheeded. My impulse was to exclaim, "Do you suppose, you
conceited young whelp, that I have taken all that trouble
and developed all that literary craft to gratify your appetite
for style? Get up at once and fetch a bucket of water; or, at
least, raise an alarm, unless you wish me to take you by the
scruff of the neck and make you do it. You call yourself a
critic: you are a mere fancier."[25]

Shaw demands that everyone take his work as seriously as
he does—and this is not always easy to do. Some people are
naturally suspicious about indicters of civilization; things
cannot really be all that bad. An indicter of civilization pats
himself on the back, for what could be more public-spirited
and heroic than pointing out the dangers that attend us?
The man who tells someone that his house is on fire deserves credit. So, Shaw implies, does he. Not everyone would
admit that his house is burning; the man who warned him
is deluded or needs glasses. Shaw rarely, if ever, admitted
this possibility. At times, Shaw's and Brecht's dicta about
themselves are similar. Each insisted on the importance of
matter over manner, each wanted to change the minds of
his audiences, not just keep them amused (although the
form of Shaw's plays is more conventional than Brecht's).
But how can one overlook "all that literary craft"? Fires are
put out sometimes without the building burning down.
In that case, the matter of the warning loses some of its
point. The manner, though, may still be admirably monosyllabic and worthy of attention. As Edmund Wilson says
in "Bernard Shaw at Eighty":

The truth is, I think, that he is a considerable artist, but that his ideas—that is, his social philosophy proper—have always been confused and uncertain. As he has grown older and as the world has been shaken out of the pattern to which he had adapted those attitudes, the inadequacy of those attitudes has been exposed.[26]

Thus are critics, from Shaw's point of view, changed to "mere fanciers."

This indicter of civilizations sometimes turned his powers of recrimination to a subject less all-encompassing, say, the theater. Shaw warned performers that he would not be just or impartial with them. In fact, a bad performance would turn him into a most unpleasant creature:

In the same way, really fine artists inspire me with the warmest personal regard, which I gratify in writing my notices without the smallest reference to such monstrous conceits as justice, impartiality, and the rest of the ideals. When my critical mood is at its height, personal feeling is not the word: it is passion: the passion for artistic perfection—for the noblest beauty of sound, sight, and action—that rages in me. Let all young artists look to it, and pay no heed to the idiots who declare that criticism should be free from personal feeling. The true critic, I repeat, is the man who becomes your personal enemy on the sole provocation of a bad performance, and will only be appeased by good performances. Now this, though well for art and for the people, means that the critics are, from the social or clubable point of view, veritable fiends.[27]

And what might his fiendish feelings have been if he had to pay for his reviewer's tickets? This practice of free tickets Shaw called "pure, unmitigated, indefensible corruption and blackmail."[28] I find no evidence that he insisted on paying for those tickets. The man who must pay for his ticket has a double frustration: a waste of time and a waste of money, whereas the reviewer wastes only time. Limited to one frustration, Shaw is giving fair warning that he will not be fair. His pleasure, or lack of it, will be translated into newsprint with no attempt at moderation. This is a risky way of doing things, a temptation for the reviewer to grow splenetic or frenetic at will. But this "passion for artistic perfection" is a Shavian passion, rooted in common sense and rationality. Although Shaw is not nearly so ponderous or sober as Dr. Johnson, some of their pronouncements have the same ring. Both of them reacted to art as if they had touched a hot stove. George Jean Nathan said that among the arts and half-arts the critic is the vainest of men, for he must "show off himself and his art at the expense of the artist and the art which he criticizes. . . . The great critics are those who, recognizing the intrinsic, permanent and indeclinable egotism of the critical art, make no senseless effort to conceal it."[29]

While reviewing music, Shaw replied to a Dr. Stanford, who had objected to hasty, prejudicial comments that journalists made about music:

> The fact is, justice is not the critic's business; and there is no more dishonest and insufferable affectation in criticism than that impersonal, abstract, judicially authoritative air which, since it is so easy to assume, and so well adapted to rapid phrase stringing, is directly encouraged by the haste which Dr Stanford deprecates.[30]

Justice is not only an illusion; it is an affectation. Shaw finds the judicial air basically dishonest; personal feelings are disguised as impartiality. For Shaw, it is more sensible to come right out and express those feelings about a performance or work of art. At least, the reader knows where the critic stands. Shaw sees no point in a critic's pretending that he has just received his opinions on Mt. Sinai. The person who says what he thinks can be met directly; the person who assumes the authoritative air is only hiding behind a smoke screen. The trouble with judicially inclined critics is that their laws may be bad more often than not. The trouble with impartial critics is that no critic really is impartial; he can only pretend to be. The upshot of the matter is, of course, that Shaw as Shaw sees him is a very fine critic. As Nathan said, "The dramatic critic who is without prejudice is on the plane with the general who does not believe in taking human life."[31]

Shaw demonstrated this "insufferable affectation" by quoting (and then adapting to his own purposes) a specimen in the prevailing style of music criticism:

> Here is the sort of thing: "The principal subject, hitherto only heard in the treble, is transferred to the bass (Ex. 28), the violins playing a new counterpoint to it instead of the original mere accompaniment figure of the first part. Then the parts are reversed, the violins taking the subject and the basses the counterpoint figure, and so on till we come to a close on the dominant of D minor, a nearly related key (commencement of Ex. 29) and then comes the passage by which we return to the first subject in its original form and key."
> How succulent this is; and how full of Mesopotamian words like "the dominant of D minor!" I will now, ladies and gentlemen, give you my celebrated "analysis" of Hamlet's soliloquy on suicide, in the same scientific style. "Shakespear, dispensing with the customary exordium, announces his subject at once in the infinitive, in which mood it is presently repeated after a short connecting passage in which, brief as it is, we recognize the alternative and negative forms on which so much of the significance of repetition depends. Here we reach a colon; and a pointed pository phrase, in which the accent falls decisively on the relative pronoun, brings us to the first full stop."[32]

For Shaw, this minute investigation of form is the equivalent of parsing.

When Shaw began to write theater reviews, he repeated his disclaimer of critical justice:

> And here let me warn the reader to carefully discount my opinion in view of the fact that I write plays myself. . . . But my criticism has not, I hope, any other fault than the inevitable one of extreme unfairness.[33]

The reader will not be gently induced into understanding. Most authors would hesitate to admit the slightest tinge of unfairness. Shaw is not only outrageous; he boasts about it. As my friend Paul Hager says about Shaw: "Supreme yet acceptable egotism."

Another statement of Shaw's intentions is in a review of a book by the actress Mary Anderson. Shaw liked the lady's book no more than the lady's acting:

> The statement that Mary Anderson was no actress is one which I am prepared to make, but not to defend. If I meet an American tourist who is greatly impressed with the works of Raphael, Kaulbach, Delaroche, and Barry, and I, with Titian and Velasquez in my mind, tell him that not one of his four heroes was a real painter, I am no doubt putting my case absurdly; but I am not talking nonsense for all that: indeed to the adept seer of pictures I am only formulating a commonplace in an irritatingly ill-considered way. But in this world if you do not say a thing in an irritating way, you may just as well not say it at all, since nobody will trouble themselves about anything that does not trouble them. The attention given to a criticism is in direct proportion to its indigestibility; and I therefore say boldly that Mary Anderson was no actress.[34]

It is impossible to mention Shaw in the same breath with the more sober and serious critics like Sidney, Coleridge, and Arnold. For a thoroughgoing rationalist, Shaw has a way of appearing outside the pale of reason. How to cope with such a man? One is tempted to take umbrage and simply dismiss him as an eccentric, and that temptation is sometimes justified. A more sensible plan is to take a Shavian remark and automatically reduce it to normal size. Buy the grains of salt by the bushelful. Shaw states that attention is directly proportional to indigestibility, but he was a vegetarian. Persons raised on more substantial nutriments are quite capable of giving undivided attention to the digestible. An irritating man will undoubtedly get attention, but that does not mean anyone will believe what he has to say. There has to be a kernel of truth in it somewhere. As Max Beerbohm said, "Shaw's judgments were often scatterbrained, but at least he had brains to scatter."[35]

The intelligence of Shaw's judgments about Shakespeare was debatable. Max objected to "that captious and rancorous spirit—inflamed, as it often seemed to me, by an almost personal animosity—in which Shaw persecuted him beyond the grave."[36] But Max hit on Shaw's great advantage: "Besides, I do not much care about good criticism. I like better the opinions of strong, narrow, creative personalities [who] are so narrow, and therefore, almost invariably, so wrong, that they are, now and again, so brilliantly right—and, always, so interesting."[37]

Shaw naturally preferred reviewers that Max would call narrow but interesting. He commends Clement Scott of the *Daily Telegraph* for writing with feeling, and condemns those who write without:

> The public believes in Mr Scott because he interprets the plays by feeling *with* the actor or author—generally more, perhaps, with the actor than the author—and giving his feeling unrestrained expression in his notices. An average young University graduate would hang himself sooner than wear his heart on his sleeve before the world as Mr Scott does. And that is just why the average young University graduate never interests anyone in his critical remarks. He has been trained to do nothing that could possibly involve error, failure, self-assertion, or ridicule; and the results of this genteelly negative policy are about as valuable as those which might be expected by a person who should enter for a swimming race with a determination to do nothing that could possibly expose him to the risk of getting wet. . . . Mr Scott, in spite of his public school education, is happily not that sort of person. He understands the value of Lassalle's dictum that "History forgives mistakes and failures, but not want of conviction."[38]

This should be inscribed for every English department.

Shaw, in arguing for the importance of conviction, overestimates Scott's personal feeling. His appreciation of the

Lyceum is mild-mannered in comparison to Shaw's attack. But attackers usually get up more steam than defenders. Shaw is praising himself as much as Clement Scott. Like Shaw's own favorite critic, Scott does not stoop to menial standards like fairness or objectivity. He immersed himself, for example, when he attacked Ibsen venomously. There Scott's convictions were put to wrongheaded purposes. Shaw admired his vehemence but often loathed his opinions. As for the "average young University graduate," Shaw could find no opinions either to loathe or admire.

Shaw's criticism is most remarkable as the work of a practicing playwright. Some might object that a playwright is too close to the theater to write dramatic criticism. Such activity requires distance, perspective, objectivity. Shaw never believed that. He found it an immense advantage to double as reviewer and playwright. One review he called "The Case for the Critic-Dramatist":

> The advantage of having a play criticized by a critic who is also a playwright is as obvious as the advantage of having a ship criticized by a critic who is also a master shipwright. Pray observe that I do not speak of the criticism of dramas and ships by dramatists and shipwrights who are not also critics; for that would be no more convincing than the criticism of acting by actors. Dramatic authorship no more constitutes a man a critic than actorship constitutes him a dramatic author; but a dramatic critic learns as much from having been a dramatic author as Shakespear or Mr Pinero from having been actors.[39]

That sounds convincing. However, a shipwright is probably a superior critic of ships for particular reasons. He may have his own ideas about construction, objecting to any other style. He is, after all, a master of the craft himself, a subjective observer with stakes in what he is criticizing. I am not familiar with any critical works by shipwrights, but there is a book by a master architect, Frank Lloyd Wright, called *The Future of Architecture*. Wright's style and impetus are remarkably like Shaw's, given the difference in subject matter. Each of them is opinionated, knowledgeable, vigorous, and immensely readable. The fault of each critic is the fault of the artist concerned about a public that will respond to his work. After reading Wright's book, I do not feel enlightened about Architecture, but I know more about the architecture of Frank Lloyd Wright. Similarly, after reading Shaw's criticism, I know less about Drama than the drama of George Bernard Shaw. He is true to his principle: "put off the learned commentator, and become a propagandist, versed in all the arts that attract a crowd, and wholly regardless of his personal dignity."[40]

Shaw the critic-dramatist offers the frankest explanation of his exhibitionism in the preface to *Three Plays for Puritans* (under the heading "On Diabolonian Ethics"). He scoffs at those who say that an author's work should stand by itself without prefaces:

> Again, they tell me that So-and-So, who does not write prefaces, is no charlatan. Well, I am. I first caught the ear of the British public on a cart in Hyde Park, to the blaring of brass bands, and this not at all as a reluctant sacrifice of my instinct of privacy to political necessity, but because, like all dramatists and mimes of genuine vocation, I am a natural-born mountebank. I am well aware that the ordinary British citizen requires a profession of shame from all mountebanks by way of homage to the sanctity of the ignoble private life to which he is condemned by his incapacity for public life. Thus Shakespear, after proclaiming that Not marble nor the gilded monuments of Princes should outlive his powerful rhyme, would apologize, in the approved taste, for making himself a motley to the view; and the British citizen has ever since quoted the apology and ignored the fanfare.[41]

Shaw maintains that his method is more direct and honest. He makes no pretensions about modesty; it is alien to his temperament:

> I write prefaces as Dryden did, and treatises as Wagner, be-

cause I *can*; and I would give half a dozen of Shakespear's plays for one of the prefaces he ought to have written. I leave the delicacies of retirement to those who are gentlemen first and literary workmen afterwards. The cart and trumpet for me.[42]

Which half-dozen, I wonder, was Shaw willing to give? If the three parts of *Henry VI, Titus Andronicus, Pericles,* and *Timon* were offered up, Shaw's exchange is reasonable. However, Shaw's sacrifice would probably include those undidactic plays he deplored very frequently, namely, *As You Like It* and *Much Ado About Nothing.*

With cart and trumpet, Shaw aimed to catch the ear of the reader as he would gain the attention of the stroller in Hyde Park. The loss of subtlety is outweighed by the gain in vigor. The audience always knows where the trumpeter stands. There is a blatant simplicity and brazen honesty about him. (G. K. Chesterton suggested that Shaw kept blowing his trumpet because it is "the one form of private property in which a Socialist can indulge.") [43] He is not fair or just, because this diminishes the liveliness of the concert. There are other attractions in the park, and the trumpeter has to make sure that his audience stays put. The midway and the platform are combined. Here is a double attraction: listening to a fine word-musician and watching a pitchman advertise his wares. The immodest modesty of Shakespeare gives way to the immodest immodesty of Shaw.

In 1931, Shaw had second thoughts about his brass-throated delivery. He wrote a postscript to "The Author's Apology," *Our Theatres in the Nineties.* He explains why his attitude to Shakespeare was so unyielding:

Let me add now what I should have added then: that a certain correction should be made, especially in reading my onslaught on Shakespear, but also in valuing my vigorous slating of my contemporaries, for the devastating effect produced in the nineties by the impact of Ibsen on the European theatre. Until then Shakespear had been conventionally ranked as a giant among psychologists and philosophers. Ibsen dwarfed him so absurdly in those aspects that it became impossible for the moment to take him seriously as an intellectual force. And if this was Shakespear's fate what could the others expect? The appearance of a genius of the first order is always hard on his competitors. Salieri said of Mozart "If this young man goes on what is to become of us?" and was actually accused of poisoning him. And certainly no one has since been just to Salieri. If my head had not been full of Ibsen and Wagner in the nineties I should have been kinder and more reasonable in my demands. Also, perhaps, less amusing. So forgive; but make the necessary allowances.[44]

A man of seventy-five recants for what he did over thirty years before. But this is a recantation in the Shavian manner. The apology is undercut: "Also, perhaps, less amusing." Despite all of Shaw's assertions that his sole purpose was to enlighten his readers, the desire to amuse played a large part. Shaw's postscript is less regretful than ironic. After all, Shaw does *not* regret his enthusiasm for Ibsen, "a genius of the first order." A "kinder and more reasonable" Shaw would have followed those standards of fairness and justice that he vehemently abjured. Shaw let fresh air into criticism. Even he might admit, though, that he sometimes left the windows open far too long.

4
Music and Thought: Shakespeare vs. Ibsen

i. The Coming of Ibsen

When Nora Helmer walks out on her husband in *A Doll's House*, audiences today remain calm. They wonder why she waited so long. Nor do they blench at syphilis in *Ghosts*. Victorian audiences recoiled with a cry of outrage when Ibsen was first performed in England; a sewer had been opened on stage. Since Shaw realized the greatness of Ibsen, the English revulsion constituted no less than an aesthetic and moral scandal. To appreciate Ibsen, the English had to change their fixed habits of mind. And the strongest habit? Shakespeare, idolized by nineteenth-century audiences, directors, and critics. Shakespeare was inviolable, but Ibsen was a violator. This situation aroused Shaw to action. Ibsen must be explained and admired. What better way than to show how Ibsen excels "Him of Avon," in G. K. Chesterton's phrase? Berating Shakespeare was not at all fair, but Shaw did not want to be fair.

Shaw tells how Ibsen struck him:

> The explanation is simple enough. Shaw's first shot at Shakespear was fired in 1894. Ibsen's first broadside on England caught the London theatre between wind and water in 1889. Shaw had written his Quintessence of Ibsenism in the meantime, and was judging everything on and off the stage by the standard set up by the terrible Norwegian. . . . Only in the Sonnets could we find Shakespear getting to the depth at which Ibsen worked.[1]

This is misleading, since Shaw never explains how Shake-

57

speare plunged to the Ibsenian depths. The preface to *The Dark Lady of the Sonnets* takes up the putative biography of Shakespeare.

Shaw found in Shakespeare some preparation for the terrible Norwegian. In *The Quintessence of Ibsenism* (1891), Shaw claims that "Shakespear survives by what he has in common with Ibsen, and not by what he has in common with Webster and the rest."[2] Ibsen makes the "spectators themselves the persons of the drama." Shakespeare did that: "The play called The Murder of Gonzago, which Hamlet makes the players act before his uncle, is artlessly constructed; but it produces a greater effect on Claudius than the Œdipus of Sophocles, because it is about himself."[3] Not even Ibsen had gone that far in hitting the nerve of the audience. *All's Well That Ends Well* has a particular luster because of "the experiment, repeated nearly three hundred years later in A Doll's House, of making the hero a perfectly ordinary young man, whose unimaginative prejudices and selfish conventionality make him cut a very fine mean figure in the atmosphere created by the nobler nature of his wife."[4] *All's Well That Ends Well, Measure for Measure,* and *Troilus and Cressida* are "those plays in which our William anticipated modern dramatic art by making serious attempts to hold the mirror up to nature."[5] (Even so, he once attacked the "vulgar pessimism" of *Troilus and Cressida*.)[6] Stage history supports Shaw's contention that *Measure for Measure* and *Troilus and Cressida,* largely neglected until the twentieth century, have a contemporary appeal. Shaw was one of the first to revive interest in these strange but powerful plays.

In 1895, Shaw wrote an article, "The Problem Play— A Symposium." In it he remarks:

At all events, we find Ibsen, after producing, in Brand, Peer Gynt, and Emperor and Galilean, dramatic poems on the grandest scale, deliberately turning to comparatively prosaic topical plays on the most obviously transitory social questions, finding in their immense magnitude under modern conditions the stimulus which, a hundred years ago, or four thousand, he would only have received from the eternal strife of man with his own spirit. A Doll's House will be as flat as ditch-water when A Midsummer Night's Dream will still be as fresh as paint; but it will have done more work in the world; and that is enough for the highest genius, which is always intensely utilitarian.[7]

How can one measure the work that a play has done in the world? How many feathers have been ruffled, how many opinions have changed, how many laws have passed? It is not easy to determine. Shaw approved of A Doll's House because it set audiences on their ears. It created a rumpus: A Midsummer Night's Dream had never done that. However, creating a rumpus is not necessarily doing work in the world. The criterion should be change, not uproar. Shaw felt that A Doll's House had changed audiences, who started to wonder whether marriages must last forever.

Shaw could have said that A Midsummer Night's Dream is a better play because it gives more pleasure, and the highest genius is always intensely aesthetic. But this would not do for Shaw the Puritan, who always opted for a stage devoted to the highest moral purpose. For Shaw, Ibsen's criticism of morality is more useful than Shakespeare's acceptance of it. Since a questioning mind is superior to a complacent one, an author who makes his readers doubt the prevailing morality deserves praise. The audience is set thinking, the first step toward change. However, over seventy years after this article, Shaw's prophecy about A Doll's House is accurate. Whatever work the play has done no longer seems significant; that is a matter for history and not sufficient cause for present enjoyment. Ibsen the utilitarian genius has lost his utility and, in this play, his vitality. Who would prefer now the ditchwater flatness of A Doll's House to the fresh paint of A Midsummer Night's Dream?

In terms of intellectual force, Ibsen the maker of docu-

ments may have an edge over Shakespeare, but Shaw sometimes let his enthusiasm run away with him. For instance,
he overestimates Gina in *The Wild Duck:* "All Shakespear's
matrons rolled into one, from Volumnia to Mrs Quickly,
would be as superficial and conventional in comparison with
Gina as a classic sibyl by Raphael with a Dutch cook by
Rembrandt."[8] Shaw does not ask: is Gina as interesting as
all those matrons rolled into one? She is only a dumpy haus-
frau. Volumnia or Mrs. Quickly has more ginger than a
score of Ginas.

Shaw could not resist donning cap and bells, even at the
expense of Ibsen. His second play, *The Philanderer* (1893),
is about London's Ibsen coterie, which compensates for its
lack of size by a show of exuberance.[9] The second and third
acts take place at the Ibsen Club. Leonard Charteris, Shaw
in thin disguise, explains the club rules: "Every candidate
for membership must be nominated by a man and a woman,
who both guarantee that the candidate, if female, is not
womanly, and if male, not manly."[10] Theory is frustrated
by fact when Grace Tranfield, one of Charteris's conquests,
refuses on Ibsenian grounds to marry him: "I will never
marry a man I love too much. It would give him a terrible
advantage over me: I should be utterly in his power. That's
what the New Woman is like. Isn't she right, Mr Philosopher?"[11] Charteris, wavering between Man and Philosopher,
takes the modern view and agrees that she is. At the curtain,
Grace has not changed her mind, and neither has he, a
philanderer still.

A prime mover in the real Ibsen coterie was William
Archer, the theater reviewer for *The World*. He made awk-
ward translations, but they were the first. Archer deserves
much credit for introducing Ibsen to England.

One way of testing Ibsen's power, Shaw said, was to translate him. Someone who knew the language of neither author
would get a better impression of Ibsen than of Shakespeare:

The foreigner can know nothing of Shakespear's power over language. He can only judge him by his intellectual force and dramatic insight, quite apart from his beauty of expression. From such a test Ibsen comes out with a double first-class: Shakespear comes out hardly anywhere.[12]

But foreigners had judged Shakespeare and not found him wanting; witness his great popularity in Germany. For Shaw, Ibsen in any language is "a thinker of extraordinary penetration, and a moralist of international influence." On the other hand, the Seven Ages of Man or "To be or not to be" is only "platitudinous fudge." Hamlet's soliloquy on suicide probably does not sound like ringing words of wisdom in translation, and Shaw's threatened translation of *Hamlet* "into modern vernacular English" did not come off.[13] On the other hand, Ibsen has sometimes sounded to foreigners like a lumbering provincial magistrate, particularly in the Archer translation that Shaw knew best.

Hesketh Pearson asked Shaw if he had met or corresponded with Ibsen. Shaw replied, "No contacts whatever."[14] Shaw never translated Ibsen. Indeed he often mentions his difficulty with languages. He did translate *Jitta's Atonement,* a play by his German translator, Siegfried Trebitsch. Shaw does not translate faithfully but hints of a happy ending alien to the original. Shaw had neither the patience nor the humility to be a translator. Besides, Shaw is not really like Ibsen, who is heavier and denser. If Shaw had translated Ibsen, the finished product would probably have been three parts Shaw to one part Ibsen.

Although with Ibsen, Shaw recognized quality, he was not so fortunate with Brieux, a French playwright who took up various social problems. The plays, if not the problems, are now happily forgotten. But Shaw went overboard in praising Brieux. In a preface to three translations (one by Mrs. Shaw), Shaw compares him favorably to Shakespeare and

Molière, who are at fault because they quarrel with God for not making men better. Brieux thinks differently:

> His fisticuffs are not aimed heavenward: they fall on human noses for the good of human souls. When he sees human nature in conflict with a political abuse, he does not blame human nature, knowing that such blame is the favorite trick of those who wish to perpetuate the abuse without being able to defend it. He does not even blame the abuse: he exposes it, and then leaves human nature to tackle it with its eyes open.[15]

In other words, Shakespeare would have served a more useful purpose if he had petitioned for old-age pensions instead of writing *King Lear*. Here Shaw's enthusiasm for Brieux the exposer of abuses leads him to think that Brieux is writing exciting plays, when in fact they are claptrap with pasteboard characters and unconvincing motivation. Shaw has value as critic of Ibsen, but he is not infallible about the new drama.

It is curious that Shaw, after numerous assaults on Shakespeare as a railer and pessimist, should have made the same charge against Ibsen, in the 1921 preface to *Back to Methuselah* (the revised preface in 1945 omits the reference to Ibsen and Strindberg) :

> The giants of the theatre of our time, Ibsen and Strindberg, had no greater comfort for the world than we: indeed much less; for they refused us even the Shakespearean-Dickensian consolation of laughter at mischief, accurately called comic relief. Our emancipated young successors scorn us, very properly. But they will be able to do no better whilst the drama remains pre-Evolutionist. Let them consider the great exception of Goethe. He, no richer than Shakespear, Ibsen, or Strindberg in specific talent as a playwright, is in the empyrean whilst they are gnashing their teeth in impotent fury in the mud, or at best finding an acid enjoyment in the irony of their predicament. Goethe is Olympian: the other giants are infernal in everything but their veracity and their repudiation

of the irreligion of their time: that is, they are bitter and hopeless.[16]

The reason for this change of emphasis is Shaw's subject: "Evolution in the Theatre." From the standpoint of a man who hoped that men would live for centuries, "the giants of the theatre of our time" must indeed have seemed short-sighted.

Ibsen *is* a bitter man (but not hopeless), although Shaw does not seem to have noticed it before. It is natural that Shaw should have recoiled somewhat from Ibsen. Shaw was the least bitter of men. He throws darts but rarely descends to the waspish. Shaw the wit would feel that Ibsen neglected comic relief. This is not always true. The bitterness of Ibsen is alleviated and undercut by humor. For example, at the end of *Hedda Gabler,* Tesman reacts to Hedda's death with his customary laugh line, "Think of that." In *The Wild Duck* Molvik the dipsomaniac is the comic relief. The fraudulent Hjalmar is funny in his illusions.

In 1925, four years after writing this preface, Shaw received the Nobel Prize. He planned to reject it but reconsidered, giving all the money for a trust fund to translate Swedish authors, particularly Strindberg, into English. Strindberg had never received a Nobel Prize, and Shaw was indignant about it. The evolutionary theater certainly had one thing in its favor; it was not averse to increasing the respect that the pre-evolutionaries deserved. Shaw met Strindberg in Stockholm. He wrote to Archer (16 July 1908) :

I achieved the impossible—a meeting with Strindberg—today. He said "Archer is not in sympathy with me." I said "Archer wasnt in sympathy with Ibsen either; but he couldnt help translating him all the same, being accessible to poetry, though otherwise totally impenetrable." After some further conversation, consisting mainly of embarrassed silence & a pale smile or two by A.S. & floods of energetic eloquence in a fearful lingo, half French, half German, by G.B.S., A.S. took out his watch & said, in German, "At two o'clock I am going to be sick." The visitors accepted this delicate intimation & withdrew.[17]

In 1933, Shaw looked back forty years, not from the evolutionary standpoint this time, and explained how he and other playwrights had reacted to the Ibsen onslaught:

> When I say that he made even Shakespear contemptible to inveterate Shakespeareans like myself his effect on the standing of lesser playwrights may be imagined. They began to write unhappy plays, and, worse still, embittered plays. They lost their ease of handling and their sense of humor. They became a prey to doubts and compunctions which they could not define: above all, they lost their lightness of heart, without which nothing can succeed in the theatre except illiterate sob-stuff and police sensation. And the ground lost in this way was not occupied by Ibsen, who soon seemed as extinct as the least lucky of the playwrights he had destroyed.[18]

Shaw was not embittered, because "an earlier enchanter had taken me far outside the bounds of middle-class idealism within which Ibsen's bombshells were deadly." The enchanter was Karl Marx. Shaw's response was not to write plays on the Ibsen model but to go back to a pre-Ibsen tradition:

> In a generation which knew nothing of any sort of acting but drawing-room acting, and which considered a speech of more than twenty words impossibly long, I went back to the classical style and wrote long rhetorical speeches like operatic solos, regarding my plays as musical performances precisely as Shakespear did.[19]

In spite of his roiling about Shakespearean music, Shaw had to admit that music's the thing. In theory, he was opposed to word-musicians; in fact, he was one himself. For instance, in *The Apple Cart* he wrote the music of politics. I held the book in my right hand and noticed that the left was doing something too; it was conducting.

ii. Shakespeare for the Ear

Shaw's knowledge of the drama, old and new, was not based on formal education. His university was the British Museum. When William Archer first saw him there, he was studying alternately a French translation of *Das Kapital* and the orchestral score of *Tristan und Isolde*. Shaw the social critic would be much less interesting if Shaw the musician had not been at work. There is a continuity of style between his music and theater reviews. Shaw did not develop his style overnight. His critical writing in the eighties and nineties improves as he goes along. The early reviews suggest what is to come, but they lack the fervor and energy that became Shaw's hallmarks. He had no difficulty in making the transition from concert hall to theater. It could not be said of him, as Dwight Macdonald said of the *New York Times*'s Howard Taubman, that he moved from the music to the theater department and began "conducting his education in public."[20]

At the instigation of A. B. Walkley, the theater reviewer for *The Times,* Shaw wrote in 1889 a review about *Richard III*. He argued that a music reviewer should do this:

> As a matter of fact, I did go to the Globe, not because Walkley wished me to hear "Mr Edward German's fine music, with its *leitmotivs* after Wagner's plan" (ha!ha!ha!), but because a musician only has the right to criticize works like Shakespear's earlier histories and tragedies. The two Richards, King John, and the last act of Romeo and Juliet, depend wholly on the beauty of their music. There is no deep significance, no great subtlety and variety in their numbers; but for splendor of sound, magic of romantic illusion, majesty of emphasis, ardor, elation, reverberation of haunting echoes, and every poetic quality that can waken the heart-stir and the imaginative fire of early manhood, they stand above all recorded music. These things cannot be spectated (Walkley signs himself Spectator): they must be heard. It is not enough to see Richard III; you should be able to *whistle* it.[21]

Every trade thinks that it is best qualified to judge the work of another. A carpenter looks at drain pipes and thinks how much better they would work installed by him instead of the plumber. So it is quite understandable that a music reviewer should look at drama and decide that the territory belongs to him. However, Shaw did not drop the idea of Shakespearean music once he became a theater reviewer. On the contrary, it is repeated constantly throughout his work for *The Saturday Review*—Shakespeare is the supreme dramatic music-maker, although the music is composed at the expense of characterization and a philosophical point of view.

Shaw's first Shakespearean review in *The Saturday Review* sets the tone for the rest.[22] He talks about a performance of *All's Well That Ends Well,* one of his favorite plays:

> What a pity it is that the people who love the sound of Shakespear so seldom go on the stage! The ear is the sure clue to him: only a musician can understand the play of feeling which is the real rarity in his early plays. In a deaf nation these plays would have died long ago. The moral attitude in them is conventional and secondhand: the borrowed ideas, however finely expressed, have not the overpowering human interest of those original criticisms of life which supply the rhetorical element in his later works. . . . In short, it is the score and not the libretto that keeps the work alive and fresh; and this is why only musical critics should be allowed to meddle with Shakespear—especially early Shakespear.

The carpenter and the plumber once more. Shaw says that Shakespeare and opera are very much alike. They may not make sense, but the tunes are nice. The aim of Shakespearean production should be to project this score, to emphasize the music. This was persistently and irritatingly ignored by theater managers:

> For the more enchanting the play is at home by the fireside in winter, or out on the heather of a summer evening—the more the manager, in his efforts to realize this enchantment by reckless expenditure on incidental music, colored lights,

dances, dresses, and elaborate rearrangements and dislocations of the play—the more, in fact, he departs from the old platform with its curtains and its placards inscribed "A street in Mantua," and so forth, the more hopelessly and vulgarly does he miss his mark. Such crown jewels of dramatic poetry as Twelfth Night and A Midsummer Night's Dream, fade into shabby colored glass in his purse; and sincere people who do not know what the matter is, begin to babble insufferably about plays that are meant for the study and not for the stage.

"Rearrangements and dislocations"—the managers think they know more than Shakespeare about writing plays. What interests them is not the score but the show, a pretty display package that leaves out the essential—the Shakespearean music. The stage managers could not do justice to Shakespeare because they had not learned to listen to him.

Shaw demonstrated how Shakespeare's music was often performed:

> The confounded thing about it is that actors, whose business it is to be experts in word music, are nearly as deaf to it as other people. At the Globe they walk in thick darkness through Shakespear's measures. They do not seem to know that Puck may have the vivacity of a street Arab, but not his voice: his bite, but never his bark; that Theseus should know all Gluck's operas by heart, and in their spirit deliver his noble lines; that Oberon must have no Piccadilly taint in his dialect to betray him into such utterances as
>
> > Be it ahnce, aw cat, aw bea-ah
> > Pahd, aw boa-ah with b'istled hai-ah
> > In thy eye that shall appea-ah
> > When thou wak'st, it is thy dea-ah.[23]

A rendition worthy of Eliza Doolittle unmetamorphosed. For Shaw, a production of Shakespeare should appeal primarily to the ear, not to the eye. Shakespearean criticism has wandered away from this emphasis on the ear. Images are sorted and labeled, and the meaning of whole plays depends on sets of interlocked metaphors. This emphasis on imagery often results in a draining away of the drama. The hunting season on metaphors is essentially an operation for the parlor and fireside, with texts spread out for viewing. Shaw's ear for Shakespearean music belongs to a man out front listening to actors.

Shaw made his opinions about Shakespearean delivery plain enough in a letter to Ellen Terry; Shakespeare is "as dead *dramatically* as a doornail":

> Your only chance of learning him without intolerable effort is to learn him by ear; for his music is unfailing. Never read your part; get somebody to speak it to you over and over again—to urge it on you, hurl it at you, until your mere imitative echo faculty forces you to jabber it as a street piano forces you to hum a tune that you positively dislike.[24]

In a letter to Mrs. Patrick Campbell, Shaw gives similar advice: "When you play Shakespear, dont worry about the character, but go for the music. It was by word music that he expressed what he wanted to express; and if you get the music right, the whole thing will come right."[25]

Shaw did not talk about Shakespearean music flippantly. He admired the score and expected that actors would give it proper consideration. In a review of *Henry IV*, Shaw advises the actor playing Hotspur how to improve:

> Would it be too far-fetched to recommend Mr Waller to study how Mozart, in rushing an operatic movement to a spirited conclusion, knew how to make it, when apparently already at its utmost, seem to bound forward by a sudden pianissimo and lightsome change of step, the speed and force of the execution being actually reduced instead of intensified by the change?[26]

At a later performance of *Julius Caesar*, Shaw spots the defects in musicianship:

> What is missing in the performance, for want of the specific Shakespearean skill, is the Shakespearean music. When we

come to those unrivalled grandiose passages in which Shake-spear turns on the full organ, we want to hear the sixteen-foot pipes booming, or, failing them (as we often must, since so few actors are naturally equipped with them), the ennobled tone, and the tempo suddenly steadied with the majesty of deeper purpose. You have, too, those moments when the verse, instead of opening up the depths of sound, rises to its most brilliant clangor, and the lines ring like a thousand trumpets.[27]

The man who could write that is not exactly averse to Shakespeare. Shaw is not concerned with minute analysis of the poetry. His point of view is an appreciative listener's with an acute ear, the amateur conductor in the fifth row center who can spot a discord a mile away.

Despite his enthusiasm, Shaw says that Shakespearean word-music has its limits:

> The fact is, there is a great deal of feeling, highly poetic and highly dramatic, which cannot be expressed by mere words—because words are the counters of thinking, not of feeling—but which can be supremely expressed by music. The poet tries to make words serve his purpose by arranging them musi-cally, but is hampered by the certainty of becoming absurd if he does make his musically arranged words mean something to the intellect as well as to the feeling.[28]

For instance, when Juliet says, "O Romeo, Romeo, where-fore art thou Romeo?" she has "to argue the case in a sort of amatory legal fashion [that] is verbally decorative; but it is not love." Shaw insists that Wagner's love-poem is better than Shakespeare's: "Romeo and Juliet with the loveliest Juliet is dry, tedious, and rhetorical in comparison with Wagner's Tristan, even though Isolde be both four-teen stone and forty, as she often is in Germany."[29] Shaw does not object that Wagner has extended "the two hours traffic of our stage" to four and a half or five. Furthermore, Isolde of the fourteen stone might grow tedious unless she could act as well as sing.

Shaw rarely tired of demonstrating that the actor-man-

agers of his time were deaf. In an essay, "On Cutting Shakespear," Shaw maintained that the managers would cut anything that did not make complete sense. That would leave
very few lines intact:

> The gayer side of Shakespear's poetic ecstasy expressed itself
> in word-dances of jingling nonsense which are, from the point
> of view of the grave Scots commentator who demands a mean-
> ing and a moral from every text, mere delirium and echolalia.
> But what would Shakespear be without them? "The spring
> time, the only merry ring time, when birds do sing hey ding a
> ding ding" is certainly not good sense nor even accurate
> ornithological observation! Who ever heard a bird sing "hey
> ding a ding ding" or anything even remotely resembling it?
> Out with it, then; and away, too, with such absurdities as
> Beatrice's obviously untrue statement that a star danced at
> her birth, which must revolt all the obstetricians and astrono-
> mers in the audience. As to Othello's fustian about the Pro-
> pontick and the Hellespont, is this senseless hullabaloo of
> sonorous vowels and precipitate consonants to be retained
> when people have trains to catch?[30]

A producer with a head for syllogisms would cut out such
passages, but a producer like Granville Barker with an ear
for music "breaks his heart in trying to get them adequately
executed." Shaw probably has an ulterior motive in staunchly
supporting the nonlogic of Shakespearean poetry. The more
he emphasizes the music, the more he shows Shakespeare's
incapacity for rational thinking. Shaw has a head for syllogisms as well as an ear for music. He takes considerable
pleasure from the music of the Propontick and the Helles-
pont; at the same time he sneers at the defective thinking
of the man who wrote it. But Shaw does not consider that
these lines characterize Othello; he may be trying to exert
self-control by taking refuge in metaphor and exact geo-
graphical reference.

Shaw is also suspect when he quotes a musical passage
from *Much Ado About Nothing*, which he called "Much
A-Doodle-Do." The Puritan in Shaw recoiled against the

banter of Beatrice and Benedick; he found it indecent. The play's advantage (and a strong one, Shaw had to admit) was the music:

> When I tell you that Benedick and the coster are equally poor in thought, Beatrice and the flower-girl equally vulgar in repartee, you reply that I might as well tell you that a nightingale's love is no higher than a cat's. Which is exactly what I do tell you, though the nightingale is the better musician.[31]

There must be some difference between Beatrice and the early Eliza Doolittle. Shaw must have known some very witty flower girls.

In light of his admiration for Ibsen, Shaw's review of *Antony and Cleopatra* is surprising.[32] The opening is familiar: "Shakespear is so much the word-musician that mere practical intelligence, no matter how well prompted by dramatic instinct, cannot enable anybody to understand his works or arrive at a right execution of them without the guidance of a fine ear." That would be high praise if one did not know the importance Shaw placed upon "mere practical intelligence." Shaw proceeds to lambaste Janet Achurch, who played Cleopatra. The objection is musical: "The lacerating discord of her wailings is in my tormented ears as I write, reconciling me to the grave." So far, this sounds typically Shavian. But then he objects again, for a different reason: "our poor Bard's historical masterpiece" has been changed to "Ibsen-and-Wagner pie." (Later Shaw admitted to finding a performance of *Hamlet* "not a bad anodyne after the anguish of the Helmer household.")[33] So this self-styled "ardent Shakespearean" cannot bear to see his favorite modernized. That is not surprising. Shaw liked Mozart too, but he did not want *Figaro* to sound like the *Ring*. Shaw did not propose that Ibsen and Wagner supplant Shakespeare. He preferred that they coexist on the stage, each performed in an appropriate way.

Two months later, Shaw went to see Miss Achurch again. His dissatisfaction had increased:

> On Monday last she was sweeping about, clothed with red Rossettian hair and beauty to match; revelling in the power of her voice and the steam pressure of her energy; curving her wrists elegantly above Antony's head as if she were going to extract a globe of gold fish and two rabbits from behind his ear; and generally celebrating her choice between the rare and costly art of being beautifully natural in lifelike human acting, like Duse, and the comparatively common and cheap one of being theatrically beautiful in heroic stage exhibition. Alas for our lost leaders! Shakespear and success capture them all.[34]

This is almost too well written. It makes me wish that I had been there to view the spectacle.

G. K. Chesterton made an ingenious suggestion about Shaw's fascination with music. The logician or arithmetician, who uses words as scientific instruments, is continually irritated by poetry. For the logician, "Music is mere beauty; it is beauty in the abstract, beauty in solution. It is a shapeless and liquid element of beauty, in which a man may really float, not indeed affirming the truth, but not denying it."[35] Although Shaw "is infinitely far above all such mere mathematicians and pedantic reasoners," his reason for liking music is not so different. It serves as an escape hatch:

> Music can be romantic without reminding him of Shakespeare and Walter Scott, with whom he has had personal quarrels. Music can be Catholic without reminding him verbally of the Catholic Church, which he has never seen, and is sure he does not like. . . . Therefore I would suggest that Shaw's love of music (which is so fundamental that it must be mentioned early, if not first, in his story) may itself be considered in the first case as the imaginative safety-valve of the rationalistic Irishman.[36]

Chesterton does not consider the possibility that the imaginative safety valve may have served too as an ego accelerator.

Shaw admired Shakespeare as musician but not as thinker, for in that department he was supposedly no match for certain other writers, Shaw, for example.

iii. The Trouble with *Othello* and *Hamlet*

Of Shakespeare's major plays, Shaw had most to say about those he quarreled with—*Othello* and *Hamlet*. *Hamlet* had the potential for the play that Shaw would have liked Shakespeare to write. But Shaw could not see much point to *Othello*, which he used as a whipping post. The most provocative essay concerns Verdi's *Falstaff* and *Otello*. After saying a few kind words for *The Merry Wives of Windsor*, Shaw starts in on *Othello*:

> The composition of Otello was a much less Shakespearean feat; for the truth is that instead of Otello being an Italian opera written in the style of Shakespear, Othello is a play written by Shakespear in the style of Italian opera. It is quite peculiar among his works in this aspect. Its characters are monsters: Desdemona is a prima donna, with handkerchief, confidante, and vocal solo all complete; and Iago, though certainly more anthropomorphic than the Count di Luna, is only so when he slips out of his stage villain's part. Othello's transports are conveyed by a magnificent but senseless music which rages from the Propontick to the Hellespont in an orgy of thundering sound and bounding rhythm; and the plot is a pure farce plot: that is to say, it is supported on an artificially manufactured and desperately precarious trick with a handkerchief which a chance word might upset at any moment. With such a libretto, Verdi was quite at home; his success with it proves, not that he could occupy Shakespear's plane, but that Shakespear could on occasion occupy his, which is a very different matter.[37]

That criticism is nothing if not challenging, even though it does sound somewhat like Rymer Revisited. It is doubtful whether the plot "is supported on an artificially manufactured and desperately precarious trick." The handkerchief is more like the straw that breaks the camel's back than the foundation of the plot. As for Iago, Shaw suggests that he spends most of his time tweaking a handlebar moustache.

Shaw jabs at *Othello* again in "A Dressing Room Secret," printed on the Haymarket Theatre program of *The Dark Lady of the Sonnets*.[38] An actor playing Iago is addressed by a bust of Shakespeare, who maintains that he "made a mess of Iago because villains are such infernally dull and disagreeable people." So Iago became instead "rather a pleasant sort of chap." The bust claims that *Othello* is a farce, "a play in which the misunderstandings are not natural but mechanical." Shakespeare has removed all reason for Othello's jealousy by "making Desdemona a decent poor devil of an honest woman, and Othello a really superior sort of man." Although the play is "nothing but wanton mischief and murder," Shakespeare says he would like to see "any of your modern chaps write anything half so good." The story ends most unhappily. The bust sneezes, explodes, and smashes to smithereens. "It never spoke again." Nor did Shakespeare's Iago, if he stuck to the promise in his last speech: "From this time forth I never will speak word."

According to Shaw, Othello is a superior sort of man and, therefore, his jealousy is not natural. But perhaps his superiority is the cause of his jealousy. He is so caught up in his rhetoric and the idea of himself as a superior creature that he is particularly vulnerable to any suggestion about a chink in his armor. Othello cares more for himself than for Desdemona. Shaw indicates this in the preface to *Getting Married;* Othello is concerned with Desdemona as property, not person: "Othello's worst agony is the thought of 'keeping a corner in the thing he loves for others' uses.' But this is not what a man feels about the thing he loves, but about the thing he owns."[39]

Shaw frequently said that the only thing interesting about *Othello* is the music. In *The Quintessence of Ibsenism,* he advanced another point of view:

It has been kept alive, not by its manufactured misunderstandings and stolen handkerchiefs and the like, nor even
by its orchestral verse, but by its exhibition and discussion
of human nature, marriage, and jealousy; and it would be a
prodigiously better play if it were a serious discussion of the
highly interesting problem of how a simple Moorish soldier
would get on with a "supersubtle" Venetian lady of fashion
if he married her. As it is, the play turns on a mistake; and
though a mistake can produce a murder, which is the vulgar
substitute for a tragedy, it cannot produce a real tragedy in
the modern sense.[40]

In other words, Shakespeare muffed an opportunity to write
about the class struggle in the home. It is hardly a theme
congenial to Shakespeare, although Shaw might have kicked
it about.

Despite his objections to the plot of *Othello,* Shaw admired the "volume of its passion and the splendor of its
word-music." What Shaw says about the poetry of *Othello*
points up his own shortcomings rather than Shakespeare's.
He picks out Othello's jealous speech, "Like to the Pontic
sea,/ Whose icy current and compulsive course/ Ne'er feels
retiring ebb," and says that this is typical of the play in
general: "The words do not convey ideas: they are stream-
ing ensigns and tossing branches to make the tempest of
passion visible."[41] So what is wrong with that? Shaw implies
that words ought to convey ideas, and if they do not, the
play is faulty. In fact, Shakespeare's words often convey
ideas, for example, when Othello makes his defense before
the council. But if the poet writes about passions, he tries
to make them visible; if he writes about ideas, he tries to
convey them. On principle, Shaw preferred ideas to passions.
He says about *Othello:* "Tested by the brain, it is ridiculous:
tested by the ear, it is sublime."[42] Shaw did not succumb
willingly to the charms of poetry.

Shaw liked to repeat what Shakespeare's bust told the
actor playing Iago—that Shakespeare's villains are very
pleasant people. In a letter to Forbes Robertson, Shaw says

that "neither Iago, Edmund, Richard nor Macbeth have any real malice in them."[43] It is true that Edmund, Iago, and Richard are fine comic characters (although it makes no sense to say that *Richard III* and *Othello,* as well as *Hamlet* and *Macbeth,* "could be changed into comedies without altering a hair of their beards").[44] They enjoy their wickedness, but that makes them no less dangerous. A really malicious person does not have to be a sourpuss. On the other hand, an audience can forget what these villains are about, because they are drawing so many laughs. Laurence Olivier's Richard is so engagingly foul that the audience's sympathies lie with him, not with the straw men he so amusingly dispatches. Richard does not really bear rancor to any of these people; they are only obstacles to be removed. But Iago detests Othello; his plans for revenge are activated by personal animus. There is real malice in him.

Shaw was somewhat kinder to *Hamlet* than to *Othello.* But the trouble is that Shakespeare, unlike Shaw, did not take the theater seriously:

> Shakespear made a few attempts, notably in Hamlet, to accuse the world of being all wrong—"out of joint," as he put it—but he attached these protests to incongruous borrowed plots and tinkerings of old plays, and never made any attempt to get down to the roots of the evil and imposture he saw everywhere. So that finally you cannot claim that Shakespear took the theatre seriously. I did; and I have been followed by some of the younger men.[45]

A comic writer like Shaw takes the theater seriously; a writer of tragedies like *Hamlet* does not. This certainly is a novel way of looking at it. Shaw complains that Shakespeare did not try to probe the morality of his time but complacently accepted it. A playwright should offer original ideas. Shakespeare was not serious because he preferred amusement to instruction. It is debatable whether Shaw's devotees now find his own instruction more nourishing than the amusement.

Shaw remarked that in *Hamlet* Shakespeare tried to accuse the world of being "out of joint." A Hamlet that refused to avenge his father would have appealed more to Shaw. Always on the alert for traces of modernism among the Elizabethans, he maintained that *Hamlet* stood at the beginning of a new movement in the drama:

> The audience finds a man in great perplexity of spirit as to what his right course of conduct should be. His duty was perfectly plain. He had come to the time when somehow or other morality was in the melting pot, and he felt that he was on uncertain ground. He felt no impulse to his duty. That was the beginning of the modern drama, which challenged moral judgment, and we must try to make the drama an instrument of continual purification and criticism of spiritual problems.[46]

What Shaw says would be correct only if *Hamlet* existed in a historical vacuum. Why was the Prince on uncertain ground? Not, as Shaw would like to think, because a proto-Ibsenian Hamlet questioned the morality of his time, but because of the Elizabethan attitudes toward ghosts and where they came from. Hamlet had to prove the story of the ghost, for it might indeed have been a "goblin damned." Hamlet rejected the chance to kill Claudius at his prayers, for then the king would go to heaven. If the elder Hamlet had been forced into purgatory, Claudius should be condemned to hell. The remark that Hamlet "felt no impulse to his duty" shows that Shaw was deficient in the historical sense. This critical fault could be turned to creative advantage. *Caesar and Cleopatra* is a remarkable play partly because Shaw gives history a decidedly modern slant.

Hamlet also interested Shaw as another round in the battle of the sexes. In the preface to *Man and Superman,* he finds that the Shavian woman acts like Ophelia and the Shakespearean heroines in general:

In Shakespear's plays the woman always takes the initiative. In his problem plays and his popular plays alike the love interest is the interest of seeing the woman hunt the man down. She may do it by charming him, like Rosalind, or by stratagem, like Mariana; but in every case the relation between the woman and the man is the same: she is the pursuer and contriver, he the pursued and disposed of. When she is baffled, like Ophelia, she goes mad and commits suicide; and the man goes straight from her funeral to a fencing match. . . . I find in my own plays that Woman, projecting herself dramatically by my hands (a process over which I assure you I have no more real control than I have over my wife), behaves just as Woman did in the plays of Shakespear.[47]

As far as Rosalind and Mariana are concerned, Shaw has a point. Rosalind cleverly manipulates Orlando (not that he needs any urging to get to the altar), and by the end of *Measure for Measure,* Angelo is disposed of, all right. As for Ophelia, nobody could believe what Shaw says (including, I suspect, Shaw). This sounds like a description of a burlesque *Hamlet* that Shaw might have tossed off. The similarity of heroines in Shakespeare and Shaw cannot be taken too seriously either. Imagine Lady Macbeth behaving just like Lady Cicely Waynflete, or Rosalind like Mrs. Warren, or Ophelia like Saint Joan. Shaw talks about "the great Shakespearean secret of always making the woman woo the man."[48] Always? Desdemona woos Othello, I suppose.

Shaw the sensible could give way to Shaw the nonsensical. When his last novel, *An Unsocial Socialist,* was not selling, he added an appendix (1887) with this *reductio ad absurdum.* It did not increase sales.

The first literary result of the foundation of our industrial system upon the profits of piracy and slavetrading was Shakespear. It is our misfortune that the sordid misery and hopeless horror of his view of man's destiny is still so appropriate to English society that we even today regard him as nor for an

age, but for all time. But the poetry of despair will not out-
live despair itself. The nineteenth-century novelists are only
the tail of Shakespear. Dont tie yourself to it: it is fast wrig-
gling into oblivion.[49]

That can be countered only by parody:

The first municipal result of the undermining of our literary
system by the accrued blasts of iconoclasm and Fabianism is
Shaw the vestryman. It is our fortune that we so far share
his meliorist view of man's destiny that we regard him as
not for a lifetime but for a term only. Shaw's beard can be
neatly trimmed by voting against him at the next election.
But as for his becoming oblivious, alas, I cannot imagine it.

The pirates-and-slaves analysis of Shakespeare was written
in 1887, several years before Shaw's campaign for Ibsen.

iv. Shakespeare Not a Thinker

In much of his criticism, Shaw tries to prove that Shakespeare was an inferior thinker in comparison with Ibsen
and Shaw. Shakespeare supposedly comes to us at a dis-
advantage because he wrote no prefaces (a felony in the
Shavian legal system). Another problem in reading Shakespeare's plays is the absence of extensive stage directions:

Of Shakespear's plays we have not even complete prompt
copies: the folio gives us hardly anything but the bare lines.
What would we not give for the copy of Hamlet used by
Shakespear at rehearsal, with the original stage business
scrawled by the prompter's pencil? And if we had in addition
the descriptive directions which the author gave on the stage:
above all, the character sketches, however brief, by which he
tried to convey to the actor the sort of person he meant him
to incarnate, what a light they would shed, not only on the
play, but on the history of the sixteenth century! . . . It is for
want of this elaboration that Shakespear, unsurpassed as poet,
storyteller, character draughtsman, humorist, and rhetorician,
has left us no intellectually coherent drama, and could not
afford to pursue a genuinely scientific method in his studies
of character and society, though in such unpopular plays as

All's Well, Measure for Measure, and Troilus and Cressida, we find him ready and willing to start at the twentieth century if the seventeenth would only let him.[50]

Shaw's own stage directions are copious. An 1894 typescript of *Arms and the Man*, with revisions in Shaw's hand, shows his method. At first the stage directions were brief to the point of curtness. Then Shaw crossed them out and on additional sheets expanded them.[51] He did this for the beginning of acts and the introduction of characters. Otherwise he made handwritten additions below, above, and to the side of the dialogue. Some of the original typed stage directions he kept; others he crossed out. He changed some dialogue too. Shaw's revised dialogue and stage directions from 1894 do not always correspond with those in the Ayot St. Lawrence Edition.

Shaw says that extensive stage directions are better than short ones; therefore, his drama is more intellectually coherent than Shakespeare's. But that does not follow. A more sensible conclusion is that Shaw's stage directions are more intellectually coherent. Of course, it would be useful if Shakespeare had provided stage directions and prompt copies. However, in a prompt copy of *Major Barbara* at the Royal Court Theatre, the diagrams and notations do not, for me, throw much light on the play.[52] There is much information about Shaw and Shavian productions. Mander and Mitchenson's *Theatrical Companion to Shaw* is very useful, listing performances and casts of Shaw's plays. But a Theatrical Companion to Shakespeare, with original dates and casts, is unthinkable. No one could disagree with Shaw in wanting to know more about the way Shakespeare's plays were acted in his own time. But when Shaw says that this lack of information results in an intellectually incoherent drama, he is only patting himself on the back again.

Nor do I see much point to "the genuinely scientific method in his studies of character and society." Shakespeare should have been a naturalist like Zola? Genuinely scientific methods are best left to scientists. Even the most modern playwrights work by intuition. What, for instance, has Shaw said about the problems of labor unionization? He has said plenty in his nondramatic prose, but in his plays very little. In fact, I doubt that a reader of his plays only would learn much about socialism. Imagine that all of Shaw's stage directions, prefaces, and essays suddenly disappeared from memory. Shaw's reputation would then have to rest on characters, plots, and dialogue. According to Shaw's own standards, his work would then be intellectually incoherent. Not everyone reads plays for that reason. If I should be deprived of Shaw's opinions on vivisection or divorce, I would not feel that one whit of damage had been done to his plays. Similarly, I cannot share Shaw's opinion that damage has been done to Shakespeare's plays by the absence of stage directions and prompt copies. Considerable damage to the knowledge of stage practice, yes, but not damage to the plays themselves.

Over the years, Shaw insisted on Shakespeare's intellectual deficiencies. By the time Shaw begin writing plays and theater reviews, he was in his middle 30s and had formed his point of view. Consequently, he kept playing variations on the same theme. He attacked Shakespeare's philosophy in the preface to *Man and Superman:*

> I read Dickens and Shakespear without shame or stint; but their pregnant observations and demonstrations of life are not co-ordinated into any philosophy or religion; on the contrary, Dickens's sentimental assumptions are violently contradicted by his observations; and Shakepear's pessimism is only his wounded humanity. Both have the specific genius of the fictionist and the common sympathies of human feeling and thought in pre-eminent degree. They are often saner and shrewder than the philosophers just as Sancho Panza was often saner and shrewder than Don Quixote. They clear away vast masses of oppressive gravity by their sense of the ridiculous, which is at bottom a combination of sound moral judgment

with lighthearted good humor. But they are concerned with the diversities of the world instead of with its unities: they are so irreligious that they exploit popular religion for professional purposes without delicacy or scruple (for example, Sydney Carton and the ghost in Hamlet!): they are anarchical, and cannot balance their exposures of Angelo and Dogberry, Sir Leicester Dedlock and Mr Tite Barnacle, with any portrait of a prophet or a worthy leader: they have no constructive ideas: they regard those who have them as dangerous fanatics: in all their fictions there is no leading thought or inspiration for which any man could conceivably risk the spoiling of his hat in a shower, much less his life.[53]

Not every playwright thinks of the theater as a guidebook for martyrs, the Whys and Wherefores of How to Lose Your Life. Shaw objects to what Hazlitt and Keats admired: the chameleon Shakespeare who could feel his way into an incredible variety of characters. Shaw would have said that a chameleon is nothing but a slippery creature that changes from one thing to another, avoiding commitment to anything.

Shaw could not be content with Shakespeare's characters. They ought to fit into some pattern or point of view. Shaw complains that Shakespeare does not project his own ideas (if he had any) into the plays; he is a creator interested only in his creations. Shaw would have little time for Keats's idea of "negative capability," because the author should be in the thick of the fray, always in evidence. The cast of characters in a Shaw play is incomplete; it omits a character that appears in all of them—Shaw, arguing, intoning, pleading. Shaw objected that Shakespeare let characters speak for themselves, existing independently of their creator; this is nothing but a yielding of responsibility, a willingness to let the story take precedence over moral purpose.

Shaw has a habit of throwing away his points; he wants to keep things spinning along without being deadly serious. What first sticks out in the passage from the *Man and Superman* preface is the man spoiling his hat in a shower. Shaw was an attention-getter, and he used every trick to get it. Unfortunately the headstands sometimes detract from the main event. Shaw does not want to get too close to what he is talking about. He can quickly withdraw by inserting a line for a laugh. Shaw is always on hand, letting the reader know what he thinks. Shakespeare is not on hand to project his personality. He remains invisible. Shaw is visible but detached, at one side mocking and jabbing.

In the preface to *Man and Superman,* the author who is praised at Shakespeare's expense is not Shaw but Bunyan, "the field preacher who achieved virtue and courage by identifying himself with the purpose of the world as he understood it." Unlike Shakespeare's heroes, Pilgrim directs his efforts toward something greater than himself; that, for Shaw, is what separates the sheep from the goats:

> This is the true joy in life, the being used for a purpose recognized by yourself as a mighty one; the being thoroughly worn out before you are thrown on the scrap heap; the being a force of Nature instead of a feverish selfish little clod of ailments and grievances complaining that the world will not devote itself to making you happy. And also the only real tragedy in life is the being used by personally minded men for purposes which you recognize to be base. All the rest is at worst mere misfortune or mortality: this alone is misery, slavery, hell on earth; and the revolt against it is the only force that offers a man's work to the poor artist, whom our personally minded rich people would so willingly employ as pandar, buffoon, beauty monger, sentimentalizer, and the like.[54]

This shows much more about Shaw than it does about Shakespeare or Bunyan. What Shaw says is somewhat puzzling, since the force in Bunyan is certainly not Nature, but God. Bunyan's guiding force is too neatly subsumed under Shaw's.

Applying Shaw's principles to Shaw, I wonder if the characters demonstrate his identification with a mighty purpose. *Back to Methuselah* indicates this, but it is unreadable. *Major Barbara* demonstrates what Shaw means. Barbara does achieve a joy in life in being used for a higher purpose. But what about Henry Higgins and Eliza Doolittle? What fervid moral purpose is evident in these characters? Shaw falls into the trap for which he blames Shakespeare, creating characters for their own sake. The trap does not make *Pygmalion* inferior to *Major Barbara*.

In 1880 Shaw wrote his second novel, *The Irrational Knot*. In the P.S. to the 1905 preface, he made his trickiest statement of Shakespeare's inferiority as a thinker. Shakespeare is a writer of the second order; Shaw belongs to the first:

Since writing the above I have looked through the proof-sheets of this book, and found, with some access of respect for my youth, that it is a fiction of the first order. By this I do not mean that it is a masterpiece in that order, or even a pleasant example of it, but simply that, such as it is, it is one of those fictions in which the morality is original and not ready-made. Now this quality is the true diagnostic of the first order in literature, and indeed in all the arts, including the art of life. It is, for example, the distinction that sets Shakespear's Hamlet above his other plays, and that sets Ibsen's work as a whole above Shakespear's work as a whole. Shakespear's morality is a mere reach-me-down; and because Hamlet does not feel comfortable in it and struggles against the misfit, he suggests something better, futile as his struggle is, and incompetent as Shakespear shews himself in his effort to think out the revolt of his feeling against ready-made morality. Ibsen's morality is original all through: he knows well that the men in the street have no use for principles, because they can neither understand nor apply them; and that what they can understand and apply are arbitrary rules of conduct, often frightfully destructive and inhuman, but at least definite rules enabling the common stupid man to know where he stands and what he may do and not do without getting into trouble. . . . By writers of the second order the ready-made morality is accepted as the basis of all moral judgment and criticism of the characters they portray, even when their genius forces them to represent their most attractive heroes and heroines as violating the ready-made code in all directions. Far be it from me to pretend that the first order is more readable than the second! Shakespear, Scott, Dickens, Dumas *père* are not, to say the least, less readable than Euripides and Ibsen. Nor is the first order always more constructive; for Byron, Oscar Wilde, and Larochefoucauld did not get further in positive philosophy than Ruskin and Carlyle, though they could snuff Ruskin's Seven Lamps with their fingers without flinching. Still, the first order remains the first order and the second the second for all that: no man who shuts his eyes and opens his mouth when religion and morality are offered to him on a long spoon can share the same Parnassian bench with those who make an original contribution to religion and morality, were it only a criticism.[55]

It takes plenty of gall to place a "novel of his nonage" in a category above Shakespeare's best work. Shaw's point, though, is familiar; Shakespeare fails to criticize the morality and religion of his time, thereby demonstrating his inferiority to Ibsen and Shaw. Shakespeare may be the better entertainer, but Shaw claims to be the better moralist and thinker.

Shaw has a point—as far as he goes. Should not literature be more than a diversion and entertainment? Should it not be a "criticism of life"? Shaw always opted for blunt didacticism. The Renaissance preferred a more subtle variety (although Shaw would have called it ephemeral). Shakespeare, like the other writers of his time, believed in "delightful teaching." Shaw's dichotomy of musician and thinker would have been inconceivable to the Renaissance. To that extent, Shaw, with his disregard for historical perspective, was guilty of misunderstanding Shakespeare's aims and technique. But it is doubtful that Shaw would have wanted to understand them. If Shakespeare had not existed, Shaw would have had to invent him, for Shakespeare was the most convenient of foils for the modern dramatists. His weaknesses, as Shaw saw them, meshed perfectly with the moderns' strengths.

Shaw's emphasis on Shakespeare's inferiority as a thinker is narrow and perverse. But the other side of the coin is Shakespeare the greatest of word-musicians. From his theater seat, Shaw listened closely. As a playwright and connoisseur of music, he took maximum interest in the way lines were spoken. Mangled Shakespeare aroused his sensibilities as much as mangled Mozart would have aroused a composer's. In the long run, Shaw is most valuable as a critic in advising not how to read, but how to produce, Shakespeare.

5
Shakespearean Production

i. Henry Irving

Shaw wrote his soundest criticism about Shakespearean production. Henry Irving was the eminent actor-manager at the Lyceum Theater. He produced twelve Shakespeare plays, 1878–1902.[1] And he was Shaw's *bête noire*. Not only did Irving refuse to perform Ibsen and Shaw, but he also committed "Bardicide." The Lyceum had enormous sets that required much time to manipulate; ten minutes to change sets could mean ten minutes cut from the text. The eye received more attention than the ear; the sets were the attraction, not the poetry. Clement Scott reported that Irving's 1896 production of *Cymbeline* would have "suggested a subject to many a painter."[2] Shaw would have retorted, "That's just the trouble."

Irving did not originate the pictorial style. Charles Kean's productions at the Princess Theatre (1850–1859) had a strong visual appeal. Many paintings of his sets are at the Victoria and Albert Museum and The Folger Shakespeare Library. Kean explained his style:

In the production of *The Merchant of Venice* it has been my object to combine with the poet's art a faithful representation of the picturesque city, to render it again palpable to the traveller who has actually gazed upon the seat of its departed glory; and at the same time, to exhibit it to the student, who has never visited this once

"More pleasant place of all festivity,
The revel of the earth, the masque of Italy."[3]

87

A prompt copy of Kean's *Hamlet* shows the graveyard scene, with a church prominently displayed.[4] The church is unnecessary, but it gives the scene painter something to do. *The Winter's Tale* is set in classical splendor, as Hermione appeals to Leontes in a vast amphitheater, and assorted Parthenons bedeck Leontes' garden.[5] The scene changes from a temple of Minerva to a room held up by caryatids, who look down on the intense melee of a dance. For processions in *Richard II*, each company of workers has its own insignia for arms and banners. The saddlers are distinct from the fishmongers, who are set off from the mercers and bakers.[6] Samuel Phelps decided that forty soldiers in his production of *Henry V* were not sufficient, but he could not afford more. Madame Tussaud modeled eighty wax heads on dummies. A rig was lashed to the waist of each soldier, who then carried a dummy on either side.[7] Thus, forty came out in triplicate.

Irving's *Merchant of Venice*, like Kean's, could educate both the untraveled student and the traveler who had gazed upon departed glory. Twenty years, off and on, Alma-Tadema worked on sets for *Coriolanus*, taking his inspiration from Etruscan tombs. A Roman sidewing, "a costermonger's stall for the sale of roasted pine cones and wine" was less funereal.[8] Irving's scene painters at the Lyceum worked on *Romeo and Juliet*. The balcony scene needs a balcony and two lovers. They are relegated to one corner; the rest of the set is filled with a garden, heavily vegetated, and a panoramic view of Verona.[9] The audience can admire simultaneously young love, botany, and Italian architecture. C. E. Montague, the reviewer for the *Manchester Guardian*, said: "Good scenepainting may be very beautiful too, but the two ways of giving background do not live well together. Mr. Hawes Craven's dawns for *Romeo and Juliet* either slay Shakespeare's or are slain by them."[10]

When Victorian photographers went to the Lyceum, they focused, at Irving's insistence, on Irving rather than the sets. Most drawings of the sets are in Irving's souvenir books for individual productions. Forbes Robertson included in the autobiography, *A Player Under Three Reigns*, his painting of the church scene in Irving's 1882 *Much Ado About Nothing*.[11] The set is nothing if not elaborate. Bulky columns are connected by lacy ironwork. A carpet to the altar rests on a polished, inlaid floor. At stage right, the altar, decorated with paintings, thrusts to the top of the stage. Censers hang, and incense is in the air. Since the reproduction of the painting is in black and white, there is no way of knowing what colors were splashed over all that architecture. It is an extraordinarily handsome set, but the words may have been lost among the columns.

From Irving's point of view, his staging was a success. It *is* undeniably impressive. The opera too had impressive staging, and Shaw insisted on the connection between opera and theater after Shakespeare. A richly illustrated book that proves Shaw's point is Hellmuth Christian Wolff's *Musikgeschichte in Bildern-Oper: Szene und Darstellung von 1600 bis 1900*. I am often reminded of the sets for Charles Kean and Henry Irving. Opera sets are gorgeous and elaborate. They give an illusion of solidity, as though an architect put them up to stay, for example, a set for Meyerbeer's *Robert le Diable* (Paris, 1831).[12] I almost think I am watching a building, not a set. Three sides of an open court are visible. Across the courtyard are three sets of arches receding into the distance: there, farther, and yet farther. A tower behind the arches is farthest. The close and the remote are in the same set.

The nineteenth-century tradition continues. At Covent Garden (1966), Luchino Visconti's sets for *Don Carlos* exaggerate perspective. The ceiling of the king's bedroom is out of proportion; it weighs down upon the walls. A peristyle is slanted so that the four sides are visible. Visconti's remarkable sets are not particularly original or modern. He is following the best nineteenth-century models for staging opera—and theater, since the styles were often indistinguish-able. In Irving's *Henry VIII*, Queen Katharine's room is not foursquare.[13] Instead, the audience looks into a corner. The two walls, of unequal length, are in the proportion of three to one. For a banqueting hall in Henry's palace, a series of arches suggests considerable space behind. The arches appear interminable. The council scene in *Hamlet* is spacious, and even more space is suggested, again by a series of arches.[14] Here space recedes in two directions; arches are both to the side and to the rear of the throne. The designer has shown one room and implied others.

At the turn of the century, *The Architectural Review* questioned the authenticity of set designs: "stage architecture is, more or less, a pot-pourri of all styles."[15] The scene painter might at least go to the nearest photographer ("one could hardly expect him to find time to visit the old build-ings themselves"). *The Architectural Review* had a more radical solution too: "To bring his work into unison with that of the poet should be the main purpose of the scenic artist; and this will hardly be done by a learned display of multitudinous detail, but rather by an effect of refined simplicity."[16] Shaw would have agreed; he did not care whether Irving's Roman costermonger's stalls were authenti-cally Roman. Were the drama and poetry authentic? Did the production appeal first to the ear, then to the eye?

According to a Lyceum program, a production of *Mac-beth* in 1889 was parceled among six acts and six scene painters.[17] The curtain rose at 7:45, and the carriages ar-rived at 11. Since this compact play required over three hours to present, a complete *Hamlet* or *Lear* would have been spun out to Wagnerian lengths. But the Lyceum had much less respect than Bayreuth for the whole work. There was not time for it, what with all those scene painters dis-playing their handiwork. Since the Restoration, there had been Shakespeare tinkerers, in particular, Nahum Tate, Colley Cibber, and David Garrick, who added and subtracted their two cents' worth. Some of these mutilations held the stage for over a century. The nineteenth-century theater managers restored some of the original scenes, but from laziness or lack of sense preferred adulterated Shakespeare to the genuine article. In his acting versions (sold in the lobby of the Lyceum), Irving deleted and rearranged but stopped short of rewriting.

Modern audiences expect fluid stage movement. Sets should be simple enough that scene follows directly on scene. In 1964 John Gielgud directed a nearly complete *Hamlet* in a little over three hours plus one intermission.[18] In Irving's time such speed was unheard of. The actor-manager Herbert Beerbohm Tree estimated that a complete *Hamlet* would take five hours.[19] When Frank Benson presented the complete *Hamlet* at the Lyceum in 1900, it took six hours and two sessions, from 3:30 to 6:30 and from 8 to 11.[20]

In his criticism, Shaw takes the playwright's point of view. In the preface to *Great Catherine,* he points out that Shakespeare provided an excessive interest for the most noted actors of the nineteenth century; they took what they needed from a dead hand. The great actors sometimes played in the "glaringly artificial high horses" written for them by Tennyson or Bulwer Lytton. The "playwrights proper" did not cater to the great actors because they "could not afford to compete with a bard who was not of an age but for all time." This led to a division between authors and actors:

> The result was that the playwrights and the great actors ceased to think of themselves as having any concern with one another: Tom Robertson, Ibsen, Pinero, and Barrie might as well have belonged to a different solar system as far as Irving was concerned; and the same was true of their respective predecessors.[21]

Who would their respective predecessors be? Shaw neglects to mention that until its closing years the nineteenth-century

English theater is dismal. He says, "For in the long run the actors will get the authors, and the authors the actors, they deserve." But there were no playwrights of quality for leading actors to perform. Therefore, it is not too surprising that they should have fallen back on Shakespeare. Although the verse drama of the nineteenth century was mostly pseudo-Shakespearean, Shaw overstates his case by claiming that Shakespeare prevented the growth of drama. A great playwright will find his actors, even though it takes time. Ibsen and Shaw are striking evidence of that. But where were the great playwrights between Sheridan and Shaw? The overexposure of Shakespeare was probably less the cause of the dry spell than a reaction to it.

When Shaw talks about his own contemporaries, he is on firmer ground. Irving did ignore Ibsen and Shaw. Yet not all the great actors ignored the new writers. Forbes Robertson took on *Caesar and Cleopatra*, and Beerbohm Tree *Pygmalion*. Shaw wrote his theater reviews in the nineties, when he was not yet popular in England. As a fledgling playwright, he had a marked interest; Irving ought to present the new drama. Polemics are not written by the rich and famous. Shaw might have been less trenchant in his reviews if he had already acquired an appreciative audience for his plays. Shaw's arguments against the Lyceum are special pleading. Without the plays of Ibsen and Shaw, his objections to Irving's stage practice lose their strength. A reviewer cannot criticize excessive playing of the old drama unless new drama of quality is available.

The Victorian actor-manager was a theatrical jack-of-all-trades, in charge of practically all aspects of production. Gordon Craig pointed out that Irving was "leader of the English stage" as well as head of the profession, that is, he was concerned both with the theater as art and as a money-making enterprise.[22] The actor-manager is now extinct, for reasons that Tyrone Guthrie explains:

Laurence Olivier, at a height of world celebrity and popularity such as Irving never attained, attempted to operate as an actor-manager at the St. James's Theatre in London. Although the policy and operations at the St. James's were far less ambitious than those at the Lyceum seventy years before, the experiment proved quite beyond the powers of a single man to sustain. This is not to say that Olivier was an ill-qualified man; far from it. He is a shrewd and capable man of prodigious energy; probably as good a businessman and a no less dedicated artist than Irving. But in the time between the two experiments the whole social, political, artistic, and financial context had changed. In almost every respect the changes have made individual enterprise, whether artistic or financial, more difficult. The day of the actor-manager has passed away, not because there is no one fit to wear the mantle of Irving, Phelps or Booth but because, with the passing of the years, the garment has become unwearable.

A general devolution of tasks has taken place. The production of a play is now undertaken by a corps of specialists. Broadly speaking, there is a business or administrative side, with a producer—in British parlance, manager—in charge; and an artistic side, headed no longer by a leading actor but by a director.[23]

Therefore, when Shaw equates the Lyceum with Irving, he is not exaggerating. A theater in the nineties approached a one-man operation.

Irving, having the final responsibility at the Lyceum, rejected Shaw's *The Man of Destiny*. This did not improve the author's disposition one bit. Not that his reputation depended on a production at the Lyceum (although it would probably have increased his popularity, which was none too high in England at that time), but how shortsighted of Irving, who preferred to play Sardou's *Madame Sans Gêne*.

In 1891, Shaw had charged in *The Quintessence of Ibsenism* that even renowned actors did not have the talents to play Ibsen. Irving, at a banquet of the Liverpool Philomathic Society, made light of the charge and of Shaw:

> It is certainly a ludicrous pretension that the fitness to play Shakespeare disqualifies an artist for embodying the creations of some dramatist who is supposed to represent a political anti-social movement. I do not know whether the Ibsen drama would obtain any permanent standing on our stage, but it is a comfort to find that, in the opinion of the author I have quoted, Shakespeare will not be entirely extinguished.[24]

If the "Ibsen drama" had depended on Irving, it would not have obtained even a temporary standing on the English stage. For that reason, Shaw continued to flail the actor. Purists might prefer that Irving's faults had been pointed out by a more objective observer whose own plays were not under consideration and who could not be accused of immodesty. But this is just what makes Shaw's observation so apt. He was in the midst of the fray, both a critic throwing darts and a playwright drawing attention to his own work. If someone complains that this was a highly prejudiced viewpoint, he is quite right. The ultimate justification for Shaw the critic is Shaw the playwright. If Shaw had written inferior plays, his reviews and essays, advertisements that they are, would have depreciated in value.

While reviewing music for *The Star,* Shaw, in a weak moment, advertised for Irving as well:

> By the way, I was at the Lyceum on Tuesday, and found Mr Irving playing very finely indeed, and quite irreproachable in my department. He and I are the only two men—not professional phonetic experts—in England who can distinguish a vowel from a diphthong.[25]

Irving was by no means irreproachable in another of Shaw's departments—dramaturgy: "Sir Henry Irving is completely independent of the dramatist, and only approaches him in moments of aberration."[26] Shaw preferred Shakespeare straight to Shakespeare diluted by Irving. Shaw did not go to the theater to watch tableaux and wait for scene changes. He did not hear the verse spoken well enough at the Lyceum, even though a vowel could be distinguished from a diphthong. Max Beerbohm admired Irving but said, "His voice could not be attuned to the glories of rhythmic cadence."[27]

Not that Shaw objected to everything he heard at the Lyceum. He was enchanted by Irving's leading lady, Ellen Terry. Shaw and Miss Terry wrote letters; Irving kept in the background, remarking about "your Mister Shaw."[28] Miss Terry and Shaw met infrequently; they preferred a friendship by mail. As Shaw said in the preface to their correspondence, "Ellen and I lived within twenty minutes of each other's doorstep, and yet lived in different worlds: she in a theatre that was a century behind the times, and I in a political society (the Fabian) a century ahead of them."[29] Ellen Terry put Shaw off his guard: she could do no wrong (or if there were any minor faults, Shaw could set them right). The Shaw-Terry letters disclose a great deal about both the writers and the theater of the time. Shaw tells Miss Terry about his plans, what he is doing and what she should be doing. He gives plentiful advice about her roles, Imogen in particular.

Some personal jealousy is behind Shaw's jabs at Irving, as Shaw makes clear in a letter to Miss Terry:

> Forgive these splenetic remarks; but really H.I.'s acting versions of Shakespear are past all bearing. The man has no artistic sense outside his own person: he is an ogre who has carried you off to his cave; and now Childe Roland is coming to the dark tower to rescue you.[30]

It is not easy to think of Shaw as a knight in shining armor. Ellen Terry certainly brought out remarkable aspects of his character.

When Shaw began his work as a theater reviewer, the Lyceum and Irving were institutions. Irving was even commemorated in the music hall by "Irving on the Brain, composed by Walter Passmore Esq., written and sung with the greatest possible success by that inimitable character comedian Edwin Barwick":[31]

> "I had a girl" until she saw The Bells.
>   Oh! Mr. Irving, you have fairly done for me;
>   Oh! Mr. Irving, you have put me up a tree;
>   You have taken my peace of mind, and left me
>   lots of pain.
>   Unnerving Henry Irving, I have got him on the brain.

There was little danger that the snipes of one reviewer would endanger the reputation or box-office receipts of a successful, unnerving concern. Irving was also a name in the United States, where he made tours with Ellen Terry. Shaw had a natural inclination to throw brickbats at people in power. Shaw attacked both the worship of The Bard and the worship of The Irving.

In his preface to the correspondence with Ellen Terry, Shaw talks about seeing Irving for the first time:

> . . . an actor with a tall thin figure, which, if it could not be convicted of grotesqueness was certainly indescribably peculiar, and a voice which was dependent so much on the resonance of a cavernous nose that it was, compared to the powerful and musical chest voice of Barry Sullivan, a highly cultivated neigh. His name was Henry Irving. I instinctively felt that a new drama inhered in this man, though I had then no conscious notion that I was destined to write it; and I perceive now that I never forgave him for baffling the plans I made for him (always, be it remembered, unconsciously).[32]

Irving's melancholy and impish humor "forced the spectator to single him out as a leading figure with an inevitability that I never saw again in any other actor until it rose from Irving's grave in the person of a nameless cinema actor who afterwards became famous as Charlie Chaplin." Shaw showed contempt for Irving's shortsighted-

ness about the modern theater, despite the adulation that
Irving received:

> From the public point of view he never looked back: from
> my point of view he never looked forward. As far as the drama
> was concerned he was more old-fashioned than the oldest of
> his predecessors, and apparently more illiterate than the most
> ignorant of them. The taste and judgment which enabled
> him to achieve so much beauty and dignity in scenery and
> costume and to rid his theatre of all the old vulgarities when
> he had Ellen Terry to reveal such possibilities to him did not
> extend to literature.[33]

As a writer, Shaw would bristle about Irving's allergy to
literature. His insistence on fidelity to the text also belongs
to him as a former music reviewer.

Even Irving's admirers admitted that his reputation was
established in spite of his personal appearance. His photographs show an unhandsome man; his face was too sharp
and angular. In later life he looked a caricature of himself,
with his incision of a mouth, severe and pouting, as if he
were clucking at somebody. He was a rather forbidding
man who might have made Richard III a chilling figure
instead of the mainly ingratiating rascal of Olivier. William
Archer said, "Once get him into the Gargoyle frame of
mind, and he is apt to rely too exclusively on sheer gro-
tesqueness of expression."[34] Archer did admit to a certain
fascination about Irving: "To me, I confess, the face under
certain aspects seems absolutely beautiful, but its beauty
is ascetic, not sensuous—a beauty not of line and curve, but
of flash and furrow."[35] But that kind of beauty did not lend
itself to certain roles, for example, Benedick, "an essentially
eupeptic personage." Irving's features were "much more
suggestive of dyspepsia." In *Romeo and Juliet,* Archer
felt, Irving would have been wise to cast himself as the
Apothecary. Ellen Terry tells of Irving's attitude toward his
physical disadvantages:

"I was thinking," he answered slowly, "how strange it is that I should have made the reputation I have as an actor, with nothing to help me—with no equipment. My legs—my voice—everything has been against me. For an actor who cant walk, cant talk, and has no face to speak of, I've done pretty well."[36]

Not so far as Shaw and Archer were concerned. Archer (with Robert W. Lowe) first attacked Irving anonymously in a shrill pamphlet, "The Fashionable Tragedian": "Mr. Irving is in fact one of the worst actors that ever trod the British stage in so-called 'leading' characters."[37] Yorick came to Irving's defense: "the admiration of a Huxley, a Gladstone, a Tennyson, and a Blackie, is not to be despised, nor the testimony of bishops to be disregarded."[38] Archer and Lowe replied: "Had the matter been one of Biology or Bulgarian atrocities, Arthurian poetry or Greek roots, the accusation would have been relevant."[39]

No one slighted The Fashionable Tragedienne. The Harvard Theatre Collection organizes Ellen Terry's photographs by role. I began with Cordelia, looking first at the photographs individually, then riffling them. Perhaps, by some kinetic sense, I could surmise how she moved on the stage. I went on to her other roles and used the same method. My conclusion: she was radiant. Since I can be charmed by photographs, consider Shaw's reaction in the audience. At fifty-eight Miss Terry played Lady Cicely Waynflete, the part in *Captain Brassbound's Conversion* that Shaw wrote for her. She looked her age, but it became her. Miss Terry's eyes were remarkable. In any role, she had a wistful look that edged into sadness. From her photographs, she is a perfect Cordelia or Desdemona but not quite at ease as Portia or Beatrice (or Lady Cicely). She had a face that could disarm a man; it certainly disarmed Shaw. She was a woman of intelligence as well as beauty. Her letters and *Memoirs* show a finely wrought mind, for example, her description of women in the days of the "exquisite wax-work," Empress Eugénie: "Oh, the beautiful *slope* of women at this period! They looked like lovely half-moons, lying back in their carriages."[40] At times her wit is worthy of her most famous correspondent; in describing the American tour with Irving, she explains why she skipped one of the sights of Chicago: "I never visited the stock-yards. Somehow I had no curiosity to see a live pig turned in fifteen minutes into ham, sausages, hair-oil, and the binding for a Bible!"[41] Her vegetarian friend would have approved.

Miss Terry played Imogen in Irving's *Cymbeline,* a production that Shaw reviewed in "Blaming the Bard." There he makes a distinction between the "interpretative actor" and the creative actor like Irving. (William Archer had made the same point over a decade before: "He creates rather than imitates. His greatest triumphs are projections of himself, not reflections of the world around him.") [42] Shaw has a grudging admiration for "the fault of a great quality—the creative quality."[43] But as a playwright he could have little patience with actors who used the author's conception of a character as a hint rather than a guideline. When Shaw argues for the interpretative actor, he is opting for the priority of the playwright. Irving was less an actor than "a rival or a collaborator who did all the real work."[44]

Shaw congratulated Irving on his impulse to "get rid of that insufferably ignorant specialist, the dramatist, and try whether something fresh cannot be done by a man equipped with all the culture of the age."[45] He made his point clear enough in another review:

This history of the Lyceum, with its twenty years' steady cultivation of the actor as a personal force, and its utter neglect of the drama, is the history of the English stage during that period. Those twenty years have raised the social status of the theatrical profession, and culminated in the official recognition of our chief actor as the peer of the President of the Royal Academy, and the figure-heads of the other arts. And

now I, being a dramatist and not an actor, want to know
when the drama is to have its turn.[46]

Gordon Craig said, in praise of Irving, "He was an actor,
and not the playwright's puppet."[47] That, for Shaw, put
the finger on the difficulty, because he did not believe that
any actor had a better dramatic sense than Shakespeare. In
the long run, the creative actor would be at fault:

> Shakespear at his highest pitch cannot be set aside by any
> mortal actor, however gifted; and when Sir Henry Irving tried
> to interpolate a most singular and fantastic notion of an old
> man between the lines of a fearfully mutilated acting version
> of King Lear, he was smashed.[48]

Shaw was willing to admit that Irving sometimes improved
on Shakespeare. Iachimo in *Cymbeline* is "a mere *diabolus
ex machina*"; Irving's Iachimo he watched "with unquali-
fied delight." But *Cymbeline* is inferior Shakespeare. Irving's
tinkering was out of place in the great roles. Gordon Craig
did not agree: "I believe that we are of the opinion that
when any man has the divine good fortune to discover that
he can act like Henry Irving, he will take whatever liberties
with whatever play he chooses, and do so with a clear conscience."[49] Shaw wants an interpretative, that is, a humble,
actor. The least humble of authors is saying that an actor
should know his place and keep it.

Shaw's own humility was put to the test by *Cymbeline,*
and was found wanting. For some weeks he had been advising Ellen Terry about Imogen. His frustration mounted.
After the performance Shaw honed his razor. He warned
Miss Terry, "I shall begin that article over again to-morrow:
it's not half nasty enough."[50] In three days came the erup-
tion:

> Pray understand, therefore, that I do not defend Cymbeline.
> It is for the most part stagey trash of the lowest melodramatic
> order, in parts abominably written, throughout intellectually

vulgar, and, judged in point of thought by modern intellectual standards, vulgar, foolish, offensive, indecent, and ex-
asperating beyond all tolerance. There are moments when
one asks despairingly why our stage should ever have been
cursed with this "immortal" pilferer of other men's stories and
ideas, with his monstrous rhetorical fustian, his unbearable
platitudes, his pretentious reduction of the subtlest problems
of life to commonplaces against which a Polytechnic debat-
ing club would revolt, his incredible unsuggestiveness, his
sententious combination of ready reflection with complete intellectual sterility, and his consequent incapacity for getting
out of the depth of even the most ignorant audience, except
when he solemnly says something so transcendently platitudinous that his more humble-minded hearers cannot bring themselves to believe that so great a man really meant to talk
like their grandmothers. With the single exception of Homer,
there is no eminent writer, not even Sir Walter Scott, whom
I can despise so entirely as I despise Shakespear when I
measure my mind against his. The intensity of my impatience
with him occasionally reaches such a pitch, that it would
positively be a relief to me to dig him up and throw stones
at him, knowing as I do how incapable he and his worshippers are of understanding any less obvious form of in-
dignity. To read Cymbeline and to think of Goethe, of
Wagner, of Ibsen, is, for me, to imperil the habit of studied
moderation of statement which years of public responsibility
as a journalist have made almost second nature in me.[51]

That is, at least, challenging. I feel, though, that a certain
defense of Shaw is in order. How many who have sneered
at this have actually spent much time with *Cymbeline,* as
Shaw had before he went to the Lyceum? I remember work-
ing on the play for only two weeks. At the end of that
frustrating period, I reread "Blaming the Bard" and found
it a model of decorum.

Henry James also saw that *Cymbeline.* Not having the
advantage of poring over the play with the leading lady,
he wrote a more sensible, if less engaging, notice:

The thing is a florid fairy-tale, of a construction so loose and
unpropped that it can scarce be said to stand upright at all,

and of a psychological sketchiness that never touches firm ground, but plays, at its better times, with an indifferent shake of golden locks, in the high, sunny air of delightful poetry. Here it disports itself beyond the reach of all challenge. Meanwhile the mere action swings, like a painted cloth in the wind, between England and Italy, flapping merrily back and forth and in and out, alternately crumpling up the picture and waving it in the blue.[52]

(And this without Shaw's advantage, as a journalist, of "studied moderation of statement.") Even so, James's attitude toward Irving is close to Shaw's. James made these pulverizing remarks in 1880, over a decade before Shaw saw red at the Lyceum:

He is what is called a picturesque actor; that is, he depends for his effects upon the art with which he presents a certain figure to the eye, rather than upon the manner in which he speaks his part. He is a thoroughly serious actor, and evidently bestows an immense deal of care and conscience upon his work; he meditates, elaborates, and, upon the line on which he moves, carries the part to a very high degree of finish. But it must be affirmed that this is a line with which the especial art of the actor, the art of utterance, of saying the thing, has almost nothing to do. Mr. Irving's peculiarities and eccentricities of speech are so strange, so numerous, so personal to himself, his vices of pronunciation, of modulation, of elocution so highly developed, the tricks he plays with the divine mother-tongue so audacious and fantastic, that the spectator who desires to be in sympathy with him finds himself confronted with a bristling hedge of difficulties. He must scramble over the hedge, as best he can, in order to get at Mr. Irving at all; to get at him, that is, as an exponent of great poetic meanings. Behind this hedge, as we may say, the actor disports himself with a great deal of ingenuity, and passes through a succession of picturesque attitudes and costumes; but we look at him only through its thorny interstices.[53]

After antagonists like Shaw and James, where could Irving find advocates as eloquent?

Shaw did give Irving credit for one thing: he had brought

acting away from Bohemia. For that, Irving patted himself on the back: "The old days when good-for-nothings passed into the profession are at an end; and the old Bohemian habits, so far as they were evil and disreputable, have also disappeared."[54] In 1895, Irving the anti-Bohemian was knighted, the first actor to be so honored. Ellen Terry later became Dame Ellen Terry.

Respectablity had its commercial advantages:

It has proved conclusive with thousands of skeptics to learn that Sir Henry Irving endorses HYOMEI.

> Lyceum Theatre
> London
> September 18, 1896

R. T. Booth, Esq.

Dear Sir:
   It is true that I am using the Booth "Hyomei" Pocket Inhaler, and I have the greatest pleasure in strongly recommending it.

> Faithfully yours,
> Henry Irving

This is the Australian "Dry-Air" treatment for Asthma, Catarrh and Bronchitis. It will break up a common cold *over night*. It "CURES BY INHALATION."[55]

As the final tribute to his respectability, Sir Henry Irving was buried in Westminster Abbey, where he rests beside Garrick under a bust of Shakespeare. Shaw refused to attend: "I returned the ticket for the Irving funeral. Literature, alas, has no place at his death as it had no place in his life. Irving would turn in his coffin if I came, just as Shakespear will turn in his coffin when Irving comes."[56]

Shaw's obituary for Irving caused much static. It was written for the *Neue Freie Presse* of Vienna. In the process of translation and retranslation, Shaw's words were mangled, and some thought he had acted in a dastardly way. The newspapers were not interested in printing Shaw's original version, which had to wait for later publication in the Ayot St. Lawrence Edition of his works. What Shaw said was neither surprising nor shocking to anyone who had read his earlier criticism of Irving. Shaw stated that Irving subordinated Shakespeare's conception to his own: "The Merchant of Venice became The Martyrdom of Irving, which was, it must be confessed, far finer than the Tricking of Shylock."[57] But Shaw had no time for his Lear, "an impertinent intrusion of a quite silly conceit of his own into a great play." In general, Irving "had no power of adapting himself to an author's conception: his creations were all his own; and they were all Irvings." Shaw imagines Shakespeare confronted with Irving at a rehearsal of *The Merchant of Venice*:

> "As I look at your playing, Sir Henry, I seem to see Israel mourning the Captivity and crying, 'How long, oh Lord, how long?' It is a little startling to see Shylock's strong feelings operating through a romantic intellect instead of through an entirely commercial one; but pray dont alter your conception, which will be abundantly profitable to us both."[58]

Shaw conveniently forgets that Shakespeare no longer received royalties.

Shakespeare might also have been startled by Irving's elaborate 1892 production of *King Lear*. He says, in the preface to his acting version, that it is set in "a time shortly after the departure of the Romans, when the Britons would naturally inhabit the houses left vacant."[59] (Macready and Phelps began the tradition of *Lear* in a Saxon setting; in 1858, Charles Kean used the "Anglo-Saxon era of the eighth century," about 300 years after the period in Irving's production.) [60]

Hawes Craven made a drawing of his design for the last scene.[61] Jutting pugnaciously skyward are approximations of the cliffs of Dover. The sea is in evidence. Ranked on either side of the stage are numerous extras costumed as fighting men with spears and lances. In an alley between the two armies, Lear and Cordelia can, with some difficulty, be seen. French critic Augustin Filon described the lighting: "In fact, evening descends, a symbolical evening; an immense cloud of blood blazes behind the rocks, and before that red light the face of the dying man stands out, very fine, mortally pale."[62] The effect was probably overwhelming, but what would have happened to the words? The words should overwhelm the sets, not vice versa. Anyone watching that production of *Lear* would have been hard pressed not to spot the cliff that beetles o'er the characters. A completely bare stage would have been preferable to chunks of simulated rock.

An inveterate theater-goer, Gordon Crosse, has described Irving's entrance as Lear:

> He is leaning on a huge scabbarded sword which he raises with a wild cry in answer to the shouted greetings of his guards. His gait, his looks, his gesture, all reveal the noble, imperious mind already degenerating into senile irritability and ready to fall into utter ruin under the coming shocks of grief and rage.[63]

Clement Scott rhapsodized, in a contradiction in terms, about the "sublimest instances of hoary senility."[64] William Poel had very different ideas about the way Lear should be played:

> He should resemble an English hunting "squarson," a man overflowing with vitality, who is as hale and active at eighty as he was at forty; a large-hearted, good-natured giant, with a face as red as a lobster. He is one of the spoilt children of nature, spoilt by reason of his favoured position in life. Responsible to no one, he thinks himself omnipotent.[65]

However, Poel never presented *Lear,* although it was his favorite play and he had spent many years in studying it.[66]

Shaw called Irving's *Lear* "fearfully mutilated." The 1892

acting version is not that bad. Of course, there is no certainty that Irving may not have made further cuts during performance. Irving's prompt copies at The Folger Shakespeare Library show that he did just that. The prompt copy of *Much Ado About Nothing* is Irving's acting version with cuts. The final scene with Dogberry and Verges is dropped.[67] This supports Shaw's contention: "Of all Sir Henry Irving's manifold treasons against Shakespear, the most audacious was his virtually cutting Dogberry out of Much Ado."[68] *Coriolanus* is mutilated. The acting version is severely cut, but the prompt copy slices even more.[69] The Folger prompt copy of *Lear* is not based on the acting version and is not cut so severely as *Much Ado* or *Coriolanus*.

Irving's acting version of *Lear* is an improvement over Nahum Tate's, which held the stage until the early nineteenth century. That trumpery, in which the fool dropped out completely, had a happy ending; Lear survived and Edgar married Cordelia. Nothing so drastic appears in Irving, nor does he try, as Tate did, to rewrite Shakespeare's lines. Most of the scenes are left intact except for the blinding of Gloucester. Irving says in the preface, "In the curtailment, all superfluous horrors have been omitted."[70] Irving also cut out the scene before the battle with Gloucester and Edgar. Thus there is no "Ripeness is all"! The interchange of Gloucester and Edgar after the pretended leap from the cliff is cut to the bone. Edgar, in his last appearance, is not given the chance to tell of his father's death or even of announcing who he is. Edmund must surely have had some curiosity about the man who felled him in single combat.

Some of Irving's cuts are judicious, the excising of lines that need many footnotes to decipher. Other times, the cuts are ridiculous and break up the rhythm of the speech. In the first scene, Kent says to Lear: "Fare thee well, King. Sith thus thou wilt appear,/ Freedom lives hence, and banishment is here." Irving cuts out the second sentence, thus neatly removing the pith.[71] Later in the same scene, Cordelia says to Lear:

>   I yet beseech your Majesty,
> If for I want that glib and oily art
> To speak and purpose not since what I well intend
> I'll do't before I speak, that you make known
> It is no vicious blot . . .

Irving's rendition is more economical: "I yet beseech your Majesty—make known/ It is no vicious blot . . ."[72] Economy here is not in the service of art. Irving does not do very well by his leading lady. Miss Terry played Cordelia, hardly the largest part in Shakespeare. She appears in only four scenes, but Irving omits one of them, her conversation with the doctor after the return from France (IV, iv).

If Shakespeare has not given Lear the final speech in the act, Irving corrects the oversight. He is usually most particular in leaving his own lines intact. However, he omits the speech on the heath that concludes, "I am a man/ More sinned against than sinning." Irving softens the play, in line with his announced intention. Therefore, Albany does not speak the stinging lines to Goneril, "Humanity must perforce prey on itself,/ Like monsters of the deep." Nor does Gloucester say, "As flies to wanton boys are we to th' gods;/ They kill us for their sport."

Irving's acting version is often irritating in what it omits, but it does not merit Shaw's remark "that if Mr Irving were to present himself in as mutilated a condition as he presented King Lear, a shriek of horror would go up from all London."[73] The cuts in *Lear* do demonstrate Shaw's point that Irving had little literary sense; he has a distressing habit of removing the best line in a speech (and sometime in a whole scene). Shaw was particularly moved to wrath in the case of *Lear*, since it was his favorite Shakespearean play. He also worried about cuts in *Cymbeline:*

In a true republic of art Sir Henry Irving would ere this have expiated his acting versions on the scaffold. He does not merely cut plays: he disembowels them. In Cymbeline he has quite surpassed himself by extirpating the antiphonal third verse of the famous dirge. A man who would do that would do anything—cut the coda out of the first movement of Beethoven's Ninth Symphony, or shorten one of Velasquez's Philips into a kitcat to make it fit over his drawing room mantelpiece.[74]

I have to take his word about the cut; the third verse is in both the acting version and the prompt copy at The Folger.

Irving justified his style of production. In the preface to Shakespeare's works, he comments on the Shakespeare tamperers: "to attempt to improve the language of our greatest dramatist is a very hopeless task."[75] (That is deceptive; omitting lines is also an attempt at improvement.) Irving then comments on his productions:

Much objection has been made to the employment of the sister arts of music and painting in the stage representation of Shakespeare, and to the elaborate illustrations of the countries in which the various scenes are laid, or of the dress and surroundings of the different characters. I do not contend that a play, fairly acted, cannot be fully effective without any of these aids and adjuncts. But, practically, their value has ceased to be a matter of opinion; they have become necessary. They are dictated by the public taste of the day—not by a desire for mere scenic display, but that demand for finish in details which has grown with the development of art in all its phases. A painter who should neglect truthful detail, however broad and powerful his method, would nowadays be exposed to severe criticism. This is not a proof of decadence; it is a striving after completeness. . . . Above all, the resources of the picturesque must be wholly subordinate to the play. . . . True criticism begins when the manager carries ornament to excess, for then he sins against the laws of beauty as well as against the poet.

Irving did not recognize Shaw's trumpetings as "true criticism."

Irving refers to objections about the other "sister art," music, a thriving enterprise in Lyceum productions. The leading composers of the day, including Arthur Sullivan, wrote background music for the Bard. Shaw had little patience with this. He did not see the point of incidental music, and he did not care for the music that was written. In a music review, Shaw predicted what would happen if things got out of hand:

> Mark my words: as actors come to understand these things better, we shall have such scenes at rehearsal as have never before been witnessed in a theatre—Rosencrantz threatening to throw up his part because his motive is half a bar shorter than Guildenstern's; the Ghost claiming, on Mozart's authority, an absolute monopoly of the trombones; Hamlet asking the composer, with magnificent politeness, whether he would mind doubling the basses with *contrafagotto* in order to bring out the Inky Cloak theme a little better; Othello insisting on being in the bass and Olivia on being in the treble when their themes are worked simultaneously with those of Iago and Viola, and the wretched composer finally writing them all in double counterpoint in order that each may come uppermost or undermost by turns.[76]

The orchestra would also play some standard musical numbers before the performance and during intermission. This did not bother Shaw. The programs for the Royal Court Theatre show that this was standard procedure for his own plays. Mozart was particularly in demand.

Shaw's malapert praise of theater reviewers can serve as a farewell to Irving.[77] The fame of an actor depends on the critics ("if it displease *them*, his credit will be interred with his bones"). Hazlitt thought that Edmund Kean was a fine actor, and now it is accepted opinion. Nor will actors' reputations go uninfluenced by Shaw:

> Some day they will reprint my articles; and then what will all your puffs and long runs and photographs and papered houses and cheap successes avail you, O lovely leading ladies

and well-tailored actor-managers? The twentieth century, if it concerns itself about either of us, will see you as I see you. Therefore study my tastes, flatter me, bribe me, and see that your acting-managers are conscious of my existence and impressed with my importance.

Smug but correct, for how does the twentieth century know what Irving's productions were like? They are largely inaccessible, in spite of drawings and photographs. We can not really see the actors move, and we can not hear them. Professor Frederick C. Packard, Jr., of Harvard has taped two Shakespearean recordings by Irving (1896): Richard III's opening speech and Buckingham's farewell from *Henry VIII*.[78] The recordings are very old and not in sufficiently good condition to evaluate Irving's delivery. There is no choice then but to fall back on the liveliest reviews about his work. What indeed if he was admired, flattered, and knighted? That is only public opinion, officialdom's stamp of approval. Irving is now seen, as predicted, through Shaw's lenses.

ii. William Poel

Shaw admired William Poel, the originator of the Elizabethan revival in staging. Poel had decided that Shakespeare's plays would work best on the stage for which they were written, not on what Shaw called the "operatic scenic peepshow stage."[79] Charles Kean and Irving had a principle for Shakespearean productions: "Spare the sets and spoil the play." Poel changed the principle to: "Raise the sets and spoil the play." Shaw emphatically agreed.

Poel did both readings and productions of Shakespeare. In 1881 his first costumed production took place on a bare, draped platform at St. George's Hall. The play was *Hamlet*, in the first quarto.[80] Robert Speaight, Poel's biographer, describes the readings in the late 1880s: "At first the actors sat round on a platform and read the plays without act or scene divisions, and with the minimum of cuts (Victorian

taste would have imposed certain omissions)."[81] Even in
his full productions, Poel emphasized the continuity of the
text; he usually left in the words and left out the gorgeous,
operatic sets. Producing *Measure for Measure* in 1893, Poel
converted the Royalty Theatre into a likeness of the Elizabethan Fortune Playhouse.[82] He alternated readings and
productions; for instance, in 1897 he did a production of
Twelfth Night, a reading of *The Merchant of Venice,* a
reading of *The Tempest,* and a production of *The Tempest.*
From 1898 on, there were few readings. Poel continued to
produce Shakespeare and the other Elizabethans until 1932,
two years before his death.

Shaw appreciated Poel's work in restoring Shakespeare to
his rightful precedence over the actor and scene painter.
Poel was no partisan of Irving. In 1877, before he produced
Shakespeare, Poel could admire in part Irving's *Richard III*:

> He has a true artistic mind, a great love for completeness in
> details of scenery and costume and correctness in the small
> parts. In his own acting he is most successful in the comedy
> element and seems to me unable to rise to greatness in a
> pathetic or passionate situation. He appears to aim at creating
> an effect by working his scene up to a striking picture upon
> which the curtain may fall. This is a modern practice that
> I much dislike as it is sensational and stagey.[83]

Forty years later, Poel, now an old hand at Shakespearean
production, had little patience with Irving and the Lyceum:

> While rejecting the declamatory methods of Macready's time,
> the actors failed by more modern means to make the characters
> alive or interesting, and to avoid tameness they were obliged
> to force their own personality into prominence instead of
> that of the characters which ought to have been impersonated.
> One of the greatest offenders in this respect was Sir Henry
> Irving, whose physical and vocal limitations made it impos-
> sible for him to do justice to many parts in which he appeared.
> His genius, however, for stage-management brought his tableau
> methods into favour, and they had many imitators, so that

managers vied with one another in the amount of money they spent on upholstery until the interest in Shakespeare's play became largely one of finance for the stage setting.[84]

Poel and Shaw saw eye to eye about Sir Henry's defects; Shaw was just as displeased that Shakespeare had become "a mere stalking-horse for the scene painter, the costumier, and the spectacular artists generally."[85] However, Poel had defects that Shaw either neglected, or was too tolerant, to mention. Robert Speaight says that he deserves immense credit for leaving Shakespeare almost intact, but he made senseless cuts and substitutions. In an 1899 production, Poel cut thirty-seven lines from Richard II's soliloquy before his murder.[86] In the 1893 production of *Measure for Measure,* Poel altered Angelo's line to Isabella about "yielding up thy body to my will"; "self" was substituted for "body." Speaight remarks: "Poel, for all his concern for accurate and musical speech, had little ear for metrical values or their reinforcement of dramatic meaning."[87] This is exactly the kind of tone-deafness for which Shaw would have pounced on Irving.

In 1890, Shaw maintained that Poel was "a much more important art propagandist than Mr Irving," for "people would know very little about Shakespear if they had no more of him than they get at the Lyceum Theatre." Shaw explains what charm Poel's experiments have for him:

> The more reason for an ordinary person like myself to avow that from these simple recitals, without cuts, waits or scenery, and therefore without those departures from the conditions contemplated by the poet which are inevitable in a modern theatre, I learn a good deal about the plays which I could learn in no other way. What is more, I enjoy myself, which is not invariably my experience in the more commercial atmosphere of the West-end theatre.[88]

Conversely Shaw the ordinary person said in the preface to *Three Plays for Puritans* that Lyceum Shakespeare disgusted him for the simple reason that he was bored. W. S. Gilbert said the same thing about plays "cut, remodelled and distorted as they are by actor-managers."[89]

In an 1895 theater review, Shaw imagines how Burbage would have reacted to the Lyceum: "he would recoil beaten the moment he realized that he was to be looked at as part of an optical illusion through a huge hole in the wall, instead of being practically in the middle of the theatre."[90] Shaw is reviewing Poel's production of *Twelfth Night* by the Elizabethan Stage Society, founded "to give practical effect to the principle that Shakespear should be accorded the build of a stage for which he designed his plays." Shaw welcomes this kind of staging, arguing that the platform stage is better for Shakespeare than the modern pictorial variety:

Years ago, comparing the effect of Much Ado as performed at the Lyceum and as read through by a number of amateurs seated in evening dress on the platform at the London Institution, I found that the amateur performance was more vivid and enjoyable, and that the illusion, though flatly contradicted by the costumes and surroundings, was actually stronger.[91]

Shaw says, "And here you have the whole secret of the Lyceum: a drama worn by age into great holes, and the holes filled up with the art of the picture gallery."[92] If Shaw had been an artist by profession, he might not have objected. As a playwright, he had no choice but to be offended.

In reviewing Poel's *Tempest,* Shaw is at his best. Again he commends Poel for letting Shakespeare, not the scene painter, create the illusion:

Mr Poel says frankly, "See that singers' gallery up there! Well, lets pretend that it's the ship." We agree; and the thing is done. But how could we agree to such a pretence with a stage ship? Before it we should say, "Take that thing away:

if our imagination is to create a ship, it must not be contradicted by something that apes a ship so vilely as to fill us with denial and repudiation of its imposture." The singing gallery makes no attempt to impose on us: it disarms criticism by unaffected submission to the facts of the case, and throws itself honestly on our fancy, with instant success. In the same way a rag doll is fondly nursed by a child who can only stare at a waxen simulacrum of infancy. A superstitious person left to himself will see a ghost in every ray of moonlight on the wall and every old coat hanging on a nail; but make up a really careful, elaborate, plausible, picturesque, blood-curdling ghost for him, and his cunning grin will proclaim that he sees through it at a glance. The reason is, not that a man can *always* imagine things more vividly than art can present them to him, but that it takes an altogether extraordinary degree of art to compete with the pictures which the imagination makes when it is stimulated by such potent forces as the maternal instinct, superstitious awe, or the poetry of Shakespear. The dialogue between Gonzalo and that "bawling, blasphemous, incharitable dog" the boatswain, would turn the House of Lords into a ship: in less than ten words—"What care these roarers for the name of king?"—you see the white horses and the billowing green mountains playing football with crown and purple.[93]

On the other hand, Irving would "multiply the expenditure enormously and spoil the illusion."

Shaw's appreciation of Poel's staging is convincing. William Archer raised a strong objection:

Nothing could have been more curious than an endeavour to realise the original presentment of *The Tempest*. But what is the first thing our Elizabethans do? They choose a side gallery or balcony, cut in the very cornice of the lofty hall, to represent the ship at sea, and they make Miranda watch the wreck from the stage, some thirty or forty feet below! Now if Shakespeare intended Miranda to be visible during the shipwreck, he would clearly place her on the raised platform at the back of the scene, looking down, as though from some headland, upon the main stage, which would represent the deck of the ship. It seems to me more probable, however, that Shakespeare intended both the lower and the upper stage to be used as parts of the ship, representing the main deck and some poop or fo'c's'le. The boatswain and mariners would appear aloft, the passengers below, and they would hail each other at some distance through the howling of the storm. This is simply my own conjecture, which must be taken for what it is worth. All we can say with absolute assurance is that Shakespeare did not picture Miranda gazing skywards, as though at Tennyson's vision of "navies grappling in the central blue." He depicts a shipwreck, not a balloon catastrophe.[94]

Archer's attack is almost as eloquent as Shaw's defense. Shaw is purposely vague about the location of the gallery ("up there"); he does not say that it was at the side of the building thirty or forty feet up, or that Miranda watched the wreck. Shaw took the broad view; he was concerned with the tendency of the production, how it differed from the style of the Lyceum. Archer was probably right as far as he went, but he did not go far enough.

Shaw makes clear that he does not always favor a rule, "the better the Shakespeare, the fewer the sets." He argues for a flexibility in staging:

It requires the nicest judgment to know exactly how much help the imagination wants. There is no general rule, not even for any particular author. You can do best without scenery in The Tempest and A Midsummer Night's Dream, because the best scenery you can get will only destroy the illusion created by the poetry; but it does not at all follow that scenery will not improve a representation of Othello. ... A great deal of the distinction of the Lyceum productions is due to the fact that Sir Henry Irving, when the work in hand is at all within the limits of his sympathies, knows exactly how far to go in the matter of scenery. When he makes mistakes, they are almost always mistakes in stage management, by which he sacrifices the effect of some unappreciated passage of dialogue of which the charm has escaped him.[95]

These are grudging words of admiration for Irving. Shaw's objection again is that Irving's deaf ear precluded a first-rate production. Shaw sees no reason for cluttering the stage with scenery in *The Tempest* or *A Midsummer Night's Dream*, because the poetry sets the scene. Why try to make the fabulous look realistic? Let the poetry do its work and give the scene painter a holiday. In Poel's productions, however, the poetry often ran up against inferior acoustics in "lofty halls," which were "too resonant for noisy speakers and too vast for gentle ones."[96] "A clean, athletic articulation" was essential.

Shaw's remarks about scenery raise questions about his own plays. *Don Juan in Hell* (without the other three acts of *Man and Superman*) was successful when Boyer, Laughton, Hardwicke, and Moorehead sat on a bare stage. To paraphrase Shaw, the best scenery available would only have destroyed the illusion created by the prose. Shaw's hell is an interplay of ideas; there is not much point in giving it a realistic appearance. On the other hand, *Saint Joan* needs sets. A king, even a king fallen on evil days, looks peculiar enthroned on a bare stage. The producer of Shaw could do what Shaw suggested about Shakespeare: think out the play beforehand and decide what style is appropriate to it, and by no means let the words play second fiddle to the scenery.

In Irving's productions, the words did not even play second fiddle; they were banished from the orchestra. In a letter to Joseph Harker, a scene painter for Irving (and later for the Forbes Robertson production of *Caesar and Cleopatra*), Shaw explained his preferences: "Now every play should be performed as its author intended it to be performed. It is no reply to this that Shakespear would have written for scenery if he could. It might as well be said that he would have written for the cinema if he could."[97] In other words, Shakespeare should be performed in Poel's manner, which was as close as possible to the Elizabethan manner. This style of production is not a new kind of scene-painting but a liberation from it:

When Mr William Poel showed that Shakespear could be played without anything that Mr Harker would call scenery, and even without anything that a Shaftesbury Avenue lessee would call a stage, and when Mr Granville Barker showed that this could be combined with stage decoration of unprecedented beauty, the old art of play presentation, in which the stage was a tribune and not a picture, revived: and it is this revival that is sometimes called advanced scene-painting. It is in fact a different art, not developed out of scene-painting, but for the moment struggling violently and occasionally abusively with it in its efforts to disentangle itself from the pictorial tradition, and win the public from its enchantments.[98]

Shaw readily admits to Harker's talents as a scene painter. But the play is more than the sets. Photographs of *Caesar and Cleopatra* show that Harker designed sets simpler than those at the Lyceum.

Not all reviewers shared Shaw's admiration for Poel. Archer said about the productions of the Elizabethan Stage Society: "Staged (more or less) after the manner of the Sixteenth Century; acted after the manner of the Nineteenth Century Amateur."[99] A. B. Walkley claimed that Poel's productions "have their place in an educational curriculum, but none in the catalogue of pleasures."[100] Max Beerbohm, in a likely thrust at Shaw, complained of "some authoritative persons" who pretend that Poel offers "the one and only dignified mode of presenting Shakespeare's plays." Max preferred to think that the "modest and sensible" Poel only tried to "pander to our passion for archaeology."[101]

Besides Shaw, C. E. Montague took Poel seriously, but he realized that Poel's productions were not authentically Elizabethan: "Mr. Poel did wonders, but he could not get rid of the proscenium arch. What he gave us was not an Elizabethan stage as it was to Elizabethan playgoers, but a picture of an Elizabethan stage seen through the frame of a modern proscenium."[102] In 1927, Poel, realizing that he had never produced a play on an open platform-stage within a theater, persuaded the management of the Holborn Empire theater to let him build out the platform over the stalls, for only one performance.[103]

Like Montague, Shaw was not blinded to Poel's faults, but he realized that Poel was on the right track in switching the emphasis from the scene painter to Shakespeare. About Poel's *Doctor Faustus* Shaw said:

> In short, Mr William Poel gave us an artistic rather than a literal presentation of Elizabethan conditions, the result being, as always happens in such cases, that the picture of the past was really a picture of the future. For which result he is, in my judgment, to be highly praised.[104]

Poel (and Shaw) have been proven correct. The picture of the past was indeed the picture of the future. Later producers, in particular Granville Barker, did not completely return to the Elizabethan manner, but they did stress a simplicity and clarity of staging quite distinct from Irving's style at the Lyceum. As Shaw said, Poel is to be highly praised, and so is Shaw for bringing attention to him.

iii. Drama Producers—Barker and Shaw

In 1885, the year Shaw began his first play, *Widowers' Houses,* he expounded on the "Qualifications of the Complete Actor." He must know "the visible symptoms of every human condition," at least those prominent on the stage:

> If a reprieve at the last moment can possibly be arranged, he should commit a murder—or even several, on persons different in sex, age, and degree of relation to himself—and get condemned to death. Burglary and forgery are experiences which no actor should be without. But study of this kind may easily be overdone. It is useless to commit outrages that are never represented on the stage, such as assaults on bishops, and the like. Child-stealing, however, should not be omitted.[105]

But Shaw's plays require a different sort of actor. No burglary or child-stealing: "Crime, like disease, is not interesting," he says in the preface to *Saint Joan.*

Shaw found his complete actor in Poel's 1899 production of *Richard II*: Harley Granville Barker. Between 1904 and 1907, Barker and J. E. Vedrenne managed the Royal Court Theatre. They presented, and Barker acted in, plays by Yeats, Maeterlinck, Schnitzler, Hauptmann, Ibsen, and Barker himself, as well as Gilbert Murray's translations of Euripides. And the two managers presented eleven Shaw plays, for a total of 701 performances.[106] This was the first concerted effort to put Shaw before English audiences. Until then, he had been less popular in England than in the tepid backwaters of the United States. At the Court, Shaw was his own producer (or, in current usage, director). Officially Barker was in charge, but actually Shaw rehearsed his own plays.

Barker is even better known for his work as Shakespearean critic and producer. He produced only three plays: *The Winter's Tale* and *Twelfth Night* in 1912, and *A Midsummer Night's Dream* in 1914. (Preliminary arrangements were made for *Macbeth* and *Antony and Cleopatra;* in 1940, Barker and Sir Lewis Casson were listed as co-producers for *King Lear,* with Gielgud.) These productions, by no means unanimously acclaimed at the time, have proven extremely influential. Shaw applauded Barker's style and described its appeal:

Mr Harley Granville-Barker, developing certain experiments made from time to time by Mr William Poel, another English-man, inaugurated twentieth century Shakespear by a series of performances in which the plays were given with unprece-dented artistic splendor without the omission of a single decently presentable line, undivided into acts, without the old pictorial scenery, and with, as a result, a blessed revelation of Shakespear as the Prince of Entertainers instead of the most dreaded of bores.[107]

Barker was primarily concerned with the play, subordinating acting and scenery to the total effect. C. B. Purdom says of

Barker: "He was a drama producer in the true sense, in contrast to the theatre producer. Irving, Tree, Boucicault, even Barrie were theatrical producers and their work may be contrasted with his."[108] In Shaw's opinion, a drama producer, not a theater producer, was the man for both Shakespeare and Shaw. Shaw the drama producer never turned his hand to Shakespeare, but he told Ellen Terry: "I am certain I could make Hamlet a success by having it played as Shakespear meant it."[109] As Shaw means it, that is.

Barker and Shaw had, according to Purdom, quite different ideas about directing actors. Shaw let out the stops; Barker toned things down: "In short, Shaw's fault was to encourage overplaying, while Barker was constantly in danger of getting underplaying."[110] Hesketh Pearson says that Barker the actor succeeded as Keegan, Marchbanks, Cusins, and Dubedat, but he was too quiet for Tanner, Valentine, Burgoyne, and Saranoff: "Shaw's long speeches, like Shakespeare's, call for the majesty and flamboyance of Barry Sullivan, Salvini and Ristori, by whom Shaw was stage-struck in his boyhood, and whom Barker had never seen."[111] Shaw said that Barker had his finger in too many pies:

> Producing kills acting: an actor's part dies if he is watching the other critically. You cannot conduct an orchestra and play the drums at the same concert. As long as I was producing and Barker acting all was well; he acted beautifully; and I took care to make the most of him.[112]

Shaw had other objections to Barker as a director; he spent too much time in rehearsal, wearing out his actors. Shaw made a rule of spending no more than three hours a day in the theater. He supports Purdom's contention that Barker underplayed:

> His only other fault was to suppress his actors when they pulled out all their stops and declaimed as Shakespear should be declaimed. They either underacted, or were afraid to act

at all lest they should be accused of ranting or being "hams." I once asked a violinist of great experience as an orchestral leader, William Reed (Elgar's Billy Reed), whether he agreed with Wagner that the first duty of a conductor is to give the right time to the band. "No," said he. "The first duty of a conductor is to let the band play." I still want the Factory Act, and hold with Billy that the perfect producer lets his actors act, and is their helper at need and not their dictator. The hint is meant specially for producers who have begun as actors. They are the first instead of the last to forget it.[113]

Barker thought differently: "Far from encouraging a company to act, a producer will need, as a rule, to prevent them from trying to, before they know what the play and the parts are about."[114] Shaw followed his own injunction against dictatorship, according to Sir Lewis Casson, Shaw's co-producer for the first English production of *Saint Joan*. However, Sir Lewis felt that Shaw sometimes went too far in letting the actors act, for they overdid the horseplay:

> The Epilogue of *Saint Joan* is a good instance. There is assuredly an intensely comic idea in the canonisation of a Saint by the Church that had burned her. But at the first production, he so overemphasized this with overplaying and funny business, that although Ernest Thesiger and I induced him to modify this considerably at rehearsal, it still shocked the audience far more than was necessary and marred the essential beauty of the play's design.[115]

I suspect that shock was exactly what Shaw wanted to produce. The alienation-effect is not the private property of Bertolt Brecht.

Sir Lewis was surprised that a professional author, who until 1904 had directed only four plays (including *Arms and the Man* in 1894), should suddenly become an accomplished director:

> How did he manage it? First, I suppose, because good actors at once recognize and respect a good actor (even if they dislike him, an impossibility in this case), and Shaw was a

mighty good actor. Whether he could have carried a characterisation through a whole evening, I don't know, but in giving a vivid half-minute sketch of a character as a demonstration, I know few better.

In *Bernard Shaw, Director*, Bernard F. Dukore says: "But Shaw was a director, not merely an acting coach. He supervised every element of production: scenery (construction and painting, as well as design), lighting, costuming, make-up—even business and house management."[116] Shaw often changed his plays for performance: "On some occasions, Shaw restored cut passages to the printed editions of his plays. . . . At other times, changes (often extensive) were incorporated in printed editions of the play."[117]

One reason that Shaw had no difficulty directing is suggested by this advice:

> When a Shakespear play is coming out—or a Sheridan one, or any old published one—buy a copy & *stage manage* it yourself, marking all the business. *Then* go and see it, and you will be astonished at the grip you will have of it & how much you will learn about the stage from your mistakes & theirs.[118]

Shaw, considering himself a playwright of Shakespearean eminence, should have acted, and not only at rehearsals. But then he would not have been content with a part as small as the Ghost or Adam. I wonder what he would have done with Don Juan, or Shotover.

Shaw, in Sir Lewis's opinion, had too leisurely an attitude about the playing time of his productions. The director kept a measured pace, in deference to the author:

> Every play consists of a series of phrases embodying ideas, mental pictures, unsatisfied questions, and so on. If the number of these ideas conveyed to an audience per minute is too low, they are bored; if high enough, they are interested. The number can be kept high either by clearly conveying every idea in turn, like shooting at a target a series of carefully aimed arrows, or by throwing handfuls of ideas at the

target at high speed, so that a fair number per minute stick and the rest are wasted. Shaw's method was certainly the former, and for plays as full of important ideas as his it is doubtless the best. But not to excess. Most of his productions at first played too slowly. Twenty minutes were saved in the case of Heartbreak House after the first night, and twenty-five of Saint Joan without cutting a word or, I think, losing any ideas.

But how were things speeded up, with Shaw's blessing or without? Shaw's lack of speed is understandable. What author would not like the audience to savor every line? The eventual speeding-up did not require cuts in the text. At the Lyceum, as Shaw describes it, a half hour of dialogue would have been disposed of so that the audience might leave the theater at the usual hour. As a music reviewer, Shaw had offered advice to directors about speed of performance:

The proper way is to divide your play into movements like those of a symphony. You will find that there are several sections which can be safely taken at a brisk *allegro,* and a few that may be taken *prestissimo:* those, for instance, which serve only to explain the mere mechanism of the plot. Each *allegro* will improve the representation if it is judiciously chosen and managed.[119]

If Shaw had directed Shakespeare, the playing time might have been drawn out in deference to the author, say, ten or fifteen minutes instead of the twenty or twenty-five for Shaw's plays.

Despite what Sir Lewis says, Shaw liked to give advice on how to gain speed in productions. In "The Art of Rehearsal," Shaw lays down this law: *"Never have a moment of silence on the stage except as an intentional stage effect."*[120] Shaw says that this is the secret of pace and of holding an audience. A play is slowed down unnecessarily if an actor stops talking while sitting or moving about the stage. Shaw rarely demonstrates humility toward actors, but here he does:

> Do not forget that though at the first rehearsal you will know more about the parts than the actors, at the last rehearsal they ought to know more about them (through their undivided attention) than you, and therefore have something to teach you about them.

I cannot recall any instance where Shaw mentions an actor who taught him something about a play, either his or Shakespeare's. Barker reinforced what he knew already.

In the preface to *Great Catherine,* Shaw speculates about Burbage's influence on Shakespeare: "Some of the difference between Shakespear's Orlandos and Bassanios and Bertrams and his Hamlets and Macbeths must have been due not only to his development as a dramatic poet, but to the development of Burbage as an actor."[121] Not that Shaw could imagine Burbage cooperating; his initial reaction to *Hamlet* would have been negative: "He denounced his part as a rotten one; thought the ghost's speech ridiculously long; and wanted to play the king."

Since Shaw stressed the absolute precedence of the author over the actor, he would not have agreed with Harold Clurman:

> For a production to have any artistic value, the play must be created afresh each time we enter the theatre. We must behave as much as possible as if we have never seen it before— which, in fact, is the truth—because Olivier's *Hamlet* is not the same play as Redgrave's or Guinness'—even though the texts are identical.[122]

Shaw went to a play with a distinct idea of what it ought to be. An inferior production was one that failed to match his point of view.

Shaw insisted that a director must be hardheaded and pay attention to specific matters of stage business; philosophizing will not do:

The notes taken by the director as he silently watches the players are a test of his competence. If, for example, he writes "Shew influence of Kierkegaard on Ibsen in this scene," or "The Œdipus complex must be very apparent here. Discuss with the Queen," the sooner he is packed out of the theatre and replaced the better. If they run "Ears too red," "Further up to make room for X," "Pleecemin," "Reel and Ideel," "Mariar Ann," "He, not Ee," "Contrast," "Change speed: Andante," "Shoe sole arches not blacked," "Unladylike: keep knees together," "More dialogue to give them time to get off," "This comes too suddenly," "?Cut this???" and the like, the director knows his job and his place.[123]

Shaw followed his principles. His own rehearsal notes are strictly logistical. Typically, Shaw's hypothetical notes include a musical suggestion, "Change speed: Andante." The note, "Unladylike: keep knees together," is credited to Shaw's cook, who pointed out that Janet Achurch was not a ladylike Cicely Waynflete: "No: she wasn't right: when she sat down she got her dress tucked in between her knees: no high lady would do that."[124] Shaw emphasizes that the director should know his place as well as his job. He should not try to lord it over the playwright, who is, or ought to be, preeminent.

The director of Shakespeare should not explain Mr. Bernard Shaw's theories about the Bard, but stick to less erudite matters:

When a play is by Shakespear such notes will crop up as "The green one red," "Tibbeeyrnottibbethat iz," "Become to Dunsinane," "Babbled," "Lo here I lenthee thishar pointed sword," meaning that the player should say "Making the green, one red," "To be? Or NOT to be? THAT is the question," "Though Birnam Wood BE come to Dunsinane," that Malone's silly "A babbled o' green fields" should be discarded for the original "His nose was as sharp as a pen on a table of green frieze," and that consecutive consonants must be articulated, as in "lend thee" and "sharp pointed." Othello must not change chaste stars into chaste tars.[125]

The director then should know the text extremely well, even the history of the text. The primary matter is how to speak the lines, how to give proper consideration to the playwright. What Shaw wants for Shakespeare is a drama producer, after Barker's model.

iv. Sullivan to Barrymore

Shaw's lifetime spanned numerous actors and styles of production. He wrote *Captain Brassbound's Conversion* and *The Millionairess* for two actresses—Ellen Terry and Katharine Hepburn—who were born sixty-two years apart! Shaw talked a great deal about the Shakespearean actors of his youth and middle-age—Sullivan, Tree, Forbes Robertson. But he took too seriously his valedictory to theater reviewing in 1898. After that, he wrote less and less about the contemporary stage.

By official opinion, Irving was the greatest Shakespearean actor of the later nineteenth century. Irving said that at Edinburgh, in 1857, he had supported Barry Sullivan's Richelieu in Bulwer Lytton's play.[126] Shaw considered Sullivan "the natural and sole successor to Burbage, Betterton, Garrick, Kemble, Kean and Macready in the British dynasty of supreme masters of their art."[127] Most actors have difficulty living up to their parts; Sullivan had difficulty finding parts that lived up to him. Shaw says that he "was a splendidly monstrous performer in his prime: there was hardly any part sufficiently heroic for him to be natural in it."[128] In 1948, Shaw wrote: "His secret, which was no secret, was simply that he presented himself as what Hamlet was: a being of a different and higher order from Laertes and the rest. He had majesty and power."[129] As Shaw said, "Hamlet's experiences simply could not have happened to a plumber."[130] However, Sullivan could not play Othello, "through which he walked as if the only line in the play that conveyed any idea to him was the description of Othello as 'perplexed in the extreme.'"[131]

SHAKESPEAREAN PRODUCTION   127

In his nineties, Shaw wrote about Sullivan's majesty and power. The article has a flavor of "Actors aren't what they used to be." However, Sullivan's acting version of *Hamlet* was by no means complete. In 1894, Shaw recounted the times he had seen *Hamlet*, but never with Fortinbras, not even in Barry Sullivan's production:

> In proof whereof, let me announce that, for all my Hamlet-going, were I to perish this day, I should go to my account without having seen Fortinbras, save in my mind's eye, or watched the ghostly twilight march (as I conceive it) of those soldiers who went to their graves like beds to dispute with him a territory that was not tomb enough and continent to hide the slain. When first I saw Hamlet I innocently expected Fortinbras to dash in, as in Sir John Gilbert's picture, with shield and helmet, like a medieval Charles XII, and by right of his sword and his will, take the throne which the fencing foil and the speculative intellect had let slip, thereby pointing the play's most characteristically English moral.[132]

After all, Fortinbras has a place in *Hamlet*, and audiences are not all that rushed to catch a train. And if they are, the curtain should just go up a half hour earlier. It indicates Shaw's admiration for Sullivan that he never attacks him, as he does Irving, for cutting the text (although he does say that Sullivan played in "old-fashioned and mutilated representations of Shakespear's plays").[133]

In the preface to the correspondence with Ellen Terry, Shaw describes Sullivan's physical appearance:

> Barry Sullivan was a tall powerful man with a cultivated resonant voice: his stage walk was the perfection of grace and dignity; and his lightning swiftness of action, as when in the last scene of Hamlet he shot up the stage and stabbed the king four times before you could wink, all provided a physical exhibition which attracted audiences quite independently of the play.[134]

Shaw does not say it here, but evidently Sullivan had better natural equipment than Irving. Even so, Shaw admitted that Sullivan "represented the grandiose and the violent on its last legs, and could do nothing for the young Irving but mislead him."[135]

Sullivan was such a perfectionist that he once apologized for a performance:

> He was as proud as Lucifer, and as imposing; but he was the only actor I ever heard come before the curtain at the end of a play to apologize for having acted badly. He had opened on Monday night in Hamlet (he was at his best in Hamlet and Richelieu) after a very rough passage from Holyhead. Certainly some of the usual charm was lacking; but only very sensitive Barry Sullivan connoisseurs could have noticed it. With an unanswerable dignity he informed the applauding Dublin playgoers that he had done justice neither to them nor to himself, and begged their indulgence. They were awestruck; and then their applause had a note of bewilderment; for most of them had thought it all very splendid.[136]

And Shaw certainly thought so too. He talks about Sullivan with boyish enthusiasm. Not even Forbes Robertson gets praise like this. Shaw may have let sentiment color his fondness for Sullivan, for Sullivan *was* the first leading actor he had ever seen, and his attachment grew.

After Sullivan, Shaw admired few Shakespearean actors. Of Irving's contemporaries, there was only one—Forbes Robertson. Other actor-managers, like Augustin Daly and Herbert Beerbohm Tree, took their share of abuse. Shaw reviewed Daly's production of *A Midsummer Night's Dream* and exploded: "At such moments, the episode of the ass's head rises to the dignity of allegory."[137] Daly regarded art as "a quaint and costly ring in the nose of Nature." The stage business made Shaw impatient:

> In my last article I was rash enough to hint that he had not quite realized what could be done with electric lighting on the stage. He triumphantly answers me by fitting up all his

fairies with portable batteries and incandescent lights, which
they switch on and off from time to time, like children with
a new toy.

The actress who played Puck evoked this comment from
him:

> . . . she announces her ability to girdle the earth in forty
> minutes in the attitude of a professional skater, and then
> begins the journey awkwardly in a swing, which takes her
> in the opposite direction to that in which she indicated her
> intention of going.

Daly's *Two Gentlemen of Verona,* Shaw said, was "founded
on Shakespear's"; Daly was "a thorough disciple of the old
school in his conviction that Shakespear was a wretchedly
unskillful dramatic author."[138]

Sir Herbert Beerbohm Tree was not a Shaw favorite
either. He contributed a remarkable essay to Max Beerbohm's collected memoirs about his brother. These circumstances are intimidating, for are not the dead to be praised
in memorial volumes? Shaw was not daunted in the least.
He did, however, admire some of Tree's stage business. In
Richard II, Tree produced striking effects with "a dog who
does not appear among Shakespear's *dramatis personae.*"
The dog licked Bolingbroke's hand, causing Richard to leave
the stage in tears. In Shakespeare, the Duke of York describes the deposed Richard's entry into London. Tree, like
Charles Kean before him, staged it impressively: "One still
remembers that great white horse, and the look of hunted
terror with which Richard turned his head as the crowd
hooted him." But Tree's delivery was something else:

> Turn now to the scenes in which Shakespear has given the
> actor a profusion of rhetoric to declaim. Take the famous
> "For God's sake let us sit upon the ground, and tell sad
> stories of the death of kings." My sole recollection of that
> scene is that when I was sitting in the stalls listening to it,
> a paper was passed to me. I opened it and read: "If you will

rise and move a resolution, I will second it.—Murray Carson."
The late Murray Carson was, above all things, an elocutionist;
and the scene was going for nothing. Tree was giving Shakespear, at immense trouble and expense, and with extraordinary
executive cunning, a great deal that Shakespear had not asked
for, and denying him something much simpler that he did ask
for, and set great store by.[139]

Tree's Malvolio was no less ingenious. He equipped four
smaller Malvolios to ape the master, in a conjunction of set
and agility:

He had a magnificent flight of stairs on the stage; and when
he was descending it majestically, he slipped and fell with a
crash sitting. Mere clowning, you will say; but no: the fall
was not the point. Tree, without betraying the smallest dis-
comfiture, raised his eyeglass and surveyed the landscape as
if he had sat down on purpose. This, like the four satellite
Malvolios, was not only funny but subtle. But when he came
to speak those lines with which any old Shakespearean hand
can draw a laugh by a simple trick of the voice, Tree made
nothing of them, not knowing a game which he had never
studied.

Hesketh Pearson said, "Indeed, the whole impersonation
left an unforgettable impression of Beerbohm Tree's Malvolio, with incidental verbal music by William Shakespeare."[140] Shaw's objections to Tree and Irving are much
alike; they subjected Shakespeare to the set designer and
stage business. Shaw objected, as a playwright would. Shaw
had not the slightest doubt that Shakespeare had more genius
than any actor or set designer.

Shaw objected again to Tree in an article, "The Dying
Tongue of Great Elizabeth":

Among the managers who are imaginative and capable enough
to count seriously, Mr Tree is the first within my experience
for whom Shakespear does not exist at all. Confronted with a
Shakespearean play, he stares into a ghastly vacuum, yet stares
unterrified, undisturbed by any suspicion that his eyesight

is failing, quite prepared to find the thing simply an ancient, dusty, mouldy, empty house which it is his business to furnish, decorate, and housewarm with an amusing entertainment. And it is astonishing how well he does it. Totally insensible to Shakespear's qualities, he puts his own qualities into the work. . . . He is always papering the naked wall, helping the lame dog over the stile, putting a gorgeous livery on the man in possession, always, like Nature, abhorring a vacuum, and filling it with the treasures of his own ingenuity and imagination and fun, and then generously giving our Shakespear the credit.[141]

Beerbohm Tree does not know his place. He is only an actor confronted with the greatest English playwright. Shaw wants a change of emphasis, not Beerbohm Tree's production of Shakespeare but Shakespeare as interpreted by his humble servant Beerbohm Tree.

In 1914, nine years after this article, Tree played Henry Higgins in the first London production of *Pygmalion* (directed by Shaw). His leading lady was Mrs. Patrick Campbell. Although Shaw carried on a celebrated friendship and correspondence with Mrs. Pat, he did not hesitate to point out her faults as woman or actress, here in a letter to Ellen Terry:

Mrs Pat Campbell entrances all London as Juliet, with a skirt dance. At the end, to shew that she is not going to give herself more trouble than she can help, she takes the dagger, and with a superb laziness, props it against the tomb and leans against the point, plainly conveying that if it will not go in on that provocation, it can let it alone. Then she lies down beside Romeo and revolves herself right over him like the roller of a mangle, leaving his sensitively chiselled profile perceptibly snubbed.[142]

Shaw said that the secret of theater reviewing was to describe. That blast at Mrs. Campbell is based loosely on description, but exaggeration by simile is more important. "The roller of a mangle" is a descriptive detail all right, but to describe an actress? The description is simple: "She takes the dagger, props it against the tomb and leans against the point. Then she lies down beside Romeo and revolves herself over him." That is what happened. But what was it like, what was the attitude of Mrs. Pat and her leading man? This requires more than description; it requires imagination and high jinks that are so amusing they seem a natural part of the description.

Shaw wrote to Mrs. Campbell and ridiculed her Lady Macbeth:

> But I couldnt understand the sleepwalking until D.D. told me someone had told you that Lady M. should be seen through a sheet of glass. I wish I had been there with a few bricks: there would not have been much left of your glass. Why do you believe every ASS who talks nonsense to you— no: why should I insult the asses?—every NOODLE who talks nonsense to you, and bite everyone who talks skilled common sense?[143]

Shaw was blessed with a temperament that recoiled from stage gimmicks.

Shaw spotted skilled common sense in Forbes Robertson. In reviewing his 1897 production of *Hamlet*, Shaw was surprised that it was "really not at all unlike Shakespear's play of the same name."[144] Shaw was so astonished to see Fortinbras in the cast of characters that he was stupefied for ten minutes. Shaw does not tell the whole story. Gordon Crosse called Forbes Robertson's *Hamlet* a "tentative, almost timid" restoration of the text.[145] Clement Scott found it strange that Forbes Robertson left in the king's prayer but omitted "that wonderful instance of Hamlet's irresolution, the sense of duty conquered by a kind heart, where he proposes to kill the King on his knees."[146] (Scott was nothing if not sentimental: "kind heart" indeed.) Archer was happy to see Fortinbras again, but could see no point in excising the soliloquy "How all occasions do inform against me."[147] As for scenic effects, the production, designed by Hawes Craven, was standard Lyceum.

Shaw overlooked the cuts in this *Hamlet* because Forbes Robertson matched Shaw's idea of what a great actor should be:

> Mr Forbes Robertson is essentially a classical actor, the only one, with the exception of Mr Alexander, now established in London management. What I mean by classical is that he can present a dramatic hero as a man whose passions are those which have produced the philosophy, the poetry, the art, and the statecraft of the world, and not merely those which have produced its weddings, coroners' inquests, and executions. And that is just the sort of actor that Hamlet requires.[148]

Another role suited him: "I wrote *Caesar and Cleopatra* for Forbes Robertson, because he is the classic actor of our day, and had a right to require such a service from me."[149] Shakespeare's Caesar is "nothing but the conventional tyrant of the Elizabethan stage"; Shaw's hero, whose passions have produced the statecraft of the world, is a role for the classic actor.

Shaw the director inveighed against silence on the stage. Shaw the reviewer admired Forbes Robertson's technique:

> He does not utter half a line; then stop to act; then go on with another half line; and then stop to act again, with the clock running away with Shakespear's chances all the time. He plays as Shakespear should be played, on the line and to the line, with the utterance and acting simultaneous, inseparable and in fact identical.[150]

Shaw said much the same thing to Ellen Terry about her Imogen:

> In playing Shakespear, play *to* the lines, *through* the lines, *on* the lines, but never between the lines. There simply isnt time for it. You should not stick five bars rest into a Beethoven symphony to pick up your drumsticks; and similarly you must not stop the Shakespear orchestra for business.[151]

Again this is a playwright's point of view. Shaw's plays often run over three hours; with actors' pauses, they would run longer than that. Shaw objects to any stage business that de-emphasizes the words. Shaw went to the theater to listen to Shakespeare; he expected his audiences to listen to Shaw, not to watch the sets. Shaw's guideline to production was "The playwright's the thing."

There is an afterpiece to this review of *Hamlet*. Several months later, the production had fallen off: "The performers had passed through the stage of acute mania, and were for the most part sleep-walking in a sort of dazed blank-verse dream."[152] This change for the worse was particularly noticeable with the Ghost, who "always comfortable, was now positively pampered, his indifference to the inconveniences of purgatory having developed into a bean-fed enjoyment of them." Shaw sees in this the danger of long runs: "instead of killing the actor, it drives him to limit himself to such effects as he can repeat to infinity without committing suicide." And *this* long run was less than three months.

I have to accept Shaw's praise of Forbes Robertson on faith, since I have heard only one recording by him (cut when he was 75) ; it does not show him to good advantage.[153] His reading of Hamlet is capricious and pinched, more appropriate for the Lord Chancellor in *Iolanthe*.

After Barker and Forbes Robertson, Shaw found little acting to admire, or even to write about. John Barrymore was the last Shakespearean actor to merit attention: "the hierarchy of great actors should be from Burbage and Betterton to Edwin Booth and Barry Sullivan. Neither Barrymore nor Irving have a place in it."[154]

In 1925, Barrymore received a letter about his production of *Hamlet*.[155] Shaw is politely devastating. After thanking Barrymore for inviting him, Shaw notes the enthusiastic audience: "Everyone felt that the occasion was one of extraordinary interest; and so far as your personality was concerned they were not disappointed." After such a beginning, Barrymore should have prepared to duck. Shaw continues with some avuncular advice about checking on the latest British methods of playing Shakespeare. *Hamlet* had recently been performed uncut at Stratford in three hours and three quarters with a ten-minute intermission. Barrymore's method was considerably different: "On Thursday last you played five minutes longer with the play cut to ribbons, even to the breath-bereaving extremity of cutting out the recorders, which is rather like playing King John without little Arthur." The hour and a half saved by cuts was filled with "an interpolated drama of your own in dumb show." This is "to take on an appalling responsibility and put up a staggering pretension":

> Shakespear, with all his shortcomings, was a very great playwright; and the actor who undertakes to improve his plays undertakes thereby to excel to an extraordinary degree in two professions in both of which the highest success is extremely rare.

Shaw talks of Shakespeare as if he were conferring an indulgence. If Barrymore lagged behind in staging, he was a little too modern in interpretation. Not only did the Œdipus complex raise its head, but there was something amiss between Laertes and Ophelia too!

Shaw repeats his injunction about acting on the line and not between the lines. Finally, he rakes Barrymore over the coals:

> I prefer my way. I wish you would try it, and concentrate on acting rather than on authorship, at which, believe me, Shakespear can write your head off. But that may be vicarious professional jealousy on my part.
>
> I did not dare to say all this to Mrs Barrymore on the night. It was chilly enough for her without a coat in the stalls without any cold water from
>
> Yours perhaps too candidly,
> G. Bernard Shaw

Shaw's ironic distaste was not shared by William Poel, who found Barrymore's *Hamlet* superior to either Irving's or Forbes Robertson's, although "the version he acts should not be called Shakespeare's *Hamlet,* but scenes from *Hamlet.*"[156] In his reverse thank-you letter, Shaw says that Barrymore's style is an aberration. Barrymore might be Irving Redivivus, taking a monitory pat on the head from Uncle George.

Shaw's letter, brilliant as it is, is dissatisfying; the militant, crusading Shaw of the nineties is now complacent about Shakespearean production, which his friend Barker, in following Poel's lead, had helped to change for the better. Much of Shaw's criticism is directed toward the faults of the stage. Once the faults were rectified, what did Shaw have to write about? In his later writing about the theater, Shaw is more concerned about conditions in the past than in the present, more concerned with repeating earlier positions than in evaluating the actors of his own day. If he had only talked about Gielgud and Olivier, and how they compared with Irving and Forbes Robertson! Like many old men, Shaw returned to the theatrical triumphs and failures of his younger days. At 92, he grew nostalgic, preferring to write about Barry Sullivan, the first eminent actor he had seen and still his favorite.

6

The Exposer Exposed

Shaw's criticism tells less about Shakespeare and Ibsen than about Shaw. He laces his writing on the theater with propaganda and self-congratulation. The criticism is less "Shakespeare as seen by Shaw" than "Shaw about Shaw via Shakespeare."

Imagine a citizen of, say, Fiji who had just read Shakespeare and looked about for a critic, say, Shaw. Unless the Fijian reader had a very strong resistance to Shaw, his attitude toward Shakespeare might be permanently warped. Shaw's criticism of Shakespeare should not be swallowed at an early age; no one should read it until a sufficient knowledge of Shakespeare has built up his immunity.

What Shaw says is valuable because he listened with a good ear. Shaw overemphasized Shakespeare the word-musician so that he could denigrate Shakespeare the nonthinker. Still, Shaw on Shakespearean music is sound and perceptive. He reveled in Shakespeare as much as in Wagner or Mozart.

Shaw admired both music and character. He says, "Rosalind is not a complete human being: she is simply an extension into five acts of the most affectionate, fortunate, delightful five minutes in the life of a charming woman."[1] One sentence is preferable to pages of detailed analysis of Rosalind. After that description, practically anything else is superfluous. Many critics of Shakespeare are self-styled devotees, yet they communicate hardly any enthusiasm. Shaw was a self-styled iconoclast, and he communicates immense enthusiasm. Shaw's criticism can be overly personal, but it is a fault in the right direction. At least, his criticism is never boring. Keeping the reader awake is not a spurious goal for criticism.

Much of Shaw's criticism was written under the pressure of a deadline. *The Saturday Review* was a weekly, so Shaw was not compelled to rap out daily reviews in the few hours between curtain and first edition. But he was not allowed long deliberations in the study. He handed in copy according to the long-standing journalistic principle that the theater is news as well as art, and the public should have it fresh. Shaw had to review many dreary plays, and he is not always in top form about them.

Highly commendable work remains. The subjects of importance are the bullying of Shakespeare and the praise of Ibsen and Shaw. Audiences now see Ibsen as Shaw saw him, a giant among playwrights. Shaw, Ibsen's champion, was instrumental in getting him a sympathetic hearing. John Gassner says there will never be another drama critic like Shaw, "for the provocation can never be duplicated. Shavian criticism was a special phenomenon of the twentieth century aborning in the nineteenth."[2]

In 1891, one year before completing his first play, *Widowers' Houses*, Shaw wrote *The Quintessence of Ibsenism*, originally a Fabian Society lecture on Socialism in Contemporary Literature. Shaw attacks ideals, "existing facts, with their masks on."[3] Ibsen is a realist, for he sees that ideals are "only swaddling clothes which man had outgrown, and which insufferably impede his movements."[4] Ibsen the destroyer of ideals is denounced as an enemy of society, though he "is in fact sweeping the world clear of lies."[5] Shaw and the Fabians had a plan for society; so, Shaw says, does Ibsen. In praising Ibsen, Shaw is drawing a blueprint. Something needs to be done; Ibsen is showing the way, to socialists and playwrights. *The Quintessence of Ibsenism* is also the call to Shaw, who talks about the technical novelties in Ibsen's plays:

first, the introduction of the discussion and its development
until it so overspreads and interpenetrates the action that it
finally assimilates it, making play and discussion practically
identical; and, second, as a consequence of making the spectators themselves the persons of the drama, and the incidents
of their own lives its incidents, the disuse of the old stage
tricks by which audiences had to be induced to take an interest
in unreal people and improbable circumstances, and the substitution of a forensic technique of recrimination, disillusion,
and penetration through ideals to the truth, with a free use
of all the rhetorical and lyrical arts of the orator, the preacher,
the pleader, and the rhapsodist.[6]

A convincing description of Shaw's dramatic technique—I
mean, Ibsen's.

Although Shaw's attitude toward Ibsen and Shakespeare
is rooted in the nineties, his flair and grace are still fasci-
nating. Now he could be read for style, not content, for the
admirable monosyllables, not the cry of "Fire!" He is clear
and incisive, at times too incisive, like the persistent re-
verberations of a power drill. His egotism is both the weakness and the strength of his criticism. Shaw boasted of his
prejudices about Shakespeare and refused to disguise his
attack. A great writer is jockeying for position at the expense
of a greater. A theatrical genius is busily carving his own
niche.

Great writers are worth listening to even when their
criticism is erratic, for it shows something about themselves.
Suppose that Shakespeare had written about Aeschylus,
Sophocles, and Euripides. (This requires a neglect of the
facts, since it is doubtful whether Shakespeare knew anything about the Greek playwrights.) Further suppose that
what he said was biased, subjective, and thoroughly un-
reliable. Would that be sufficient reason for not reading
what he had to say? Of course not, since Shakespeare would
have written it and might well have shown more about himself than about the Greeks. Shakespeare's criticism might
not make classical scholars happy, but it would give pleasure

to an ardent Shakespearean. Shaw about Shakespeare will always be read with enthusiasm by devotees of Shaw. Those who like Shakespeare but not Shaw may object.

Throughout his criticism, Shaw makes certain assumptions about himself, what kind of writer he is, and how he differs from Shakespeare. An important argument (see close of chapter 4 above) is set down in the P.S. to the preface of his second novel, *The Irrational Knot*. There Shaw makes his distinction between writers of the first and second order. The writers of the second order accept the morality of their time "as the basis of all moral judgments and criticism of the characters they portray." The writers of the first order "make an original contribution to religion and morality, were it only a criticism." Shakespeare is a writer of the second order, Ibsen and Shaw of the first. Although denying that writers of the first order are more readable, Shaw still asserts that they are a superior breed. He has put himself in a compartment right over Shakespeare. For the sake of neat pigeonholing, Shaw has asserted his right and Ibsen's to be taken more seriously than Shakespeare.

In *The Intelligent Woman's Guide to Socialism and Capitalism*, Shaw repeats his claim:

> I am myself by profession what is called an original thinker, my business being to question and test all the established creeds and codes to see how far they are still valid and how far worn out or superseded, and even to draft new creeds and codes.[7]

By his own definition, Shaw is certainly an original thinker. He devoted his life to testing the established creeds and codes. The purpose of the Fabian Society was to do just that. Shaw attacks the social organization of England and proposes a socialist state to replace it. The Fabian Society now seems eminently respectable, since it was essential in the founding of the Labor Party. In the 1890s their moderate socialist ideas were not accepted by most people. The

Fabians, as far as public opinion went, were outlandish, and Shaw was the most outlandish of all. He devoted much time to advocating unpopular authors, for example, Marx and Nietzsche.

But Shaw's definition of original thinker is special. The usual definition would be: a man who concocts his own ideas. Shaw does not claim that; he insists that his ideas criticize the morality of the time.

What is the source of those ideas? Does Shaw concoct, or does he borrow? An extremely clever assimilator of other men's ideas, Shaw read voraciously in literature, history, and economics. His own thinking is a dish of leftovers—expertly prepared, to be sure: a generous helping of reconstituted Marx, a few cups of warmed-over Samuel Butler, several cutlets of reheated Nietzsche. The casserole is savory, but the intellectual ingredients are not fresh from the market.

In the preface to *Three Plays for Puritans,* Shaw says this himself:

> It is a dangerous thing to be hailed at once, as a few rash admirers have hailed me, as above all things original: what the world calls originality is only an unaccustomed method of tickling it. Meyerbeer seemed prodigiously original to the Parisians when he first burst on them. Today, he is only the crow who followed Beethoven's plough. I am a crow who have followed many ploughs. No doubt I seem prodigiously clever to those who have never hopped, hungry and curious, across the fields of philosophy, politics, and art.[8]

Is Shaw contradicting himself by saying he is not original? No, but he is swinging between the two definitions of "original thinker," his own and the usual, between "tester of creeds and codes" and "concocter of one's own ideas." By his own definition, Shaw says that he is an original thinker. However, by the second definition, Shaw says that he is not an original thinker, for "I am a crow who have followed many ploughs." From Shaw's perspective he can be both an original thinker rejecting the morality of his time in favor of new creeds and codes and an unoriginal assimilator filching from Marx, Butler, and Nietzsche.

Someone said of Browning there was always a danger of mistaking him for a philosopher. The same can be said of Shaw. He persistently avows the superiority of his content to his form, of matter to manner, of message to delivery. Today he is not so much an agitated renovator of society as a playwright whose works are remarkably graceful and energetic. He is prodigiously clever not because of his hungry and curious hopping, but because his characters and dialogue are first-rate.

Shaw lumps an assortment of authors under the first order: Euripides, La Rochefoucauld, Byron, Wilde, Ibsen. None of them was technically a philosopher. All of them, however, saw through the societies they lived in and made trenchant artistic points about them. For Shaw, originality is first a naysaying and a rejection; the writer of the second order assents to and accepts the world. The writer of the first order is original even if he makes only a criticism of religion and morality. Shaw was not content with criticism alone. He proposed substitute standards of behavior. He said not only, "You're wrong," but also, "Here is what you must do." And England must follow the Fabian standard.

Shaw of the first order objected loud and long to Shakespeare as a snapper-up of unconsidered philosophical trifles. Shakespeare was too much a man of his time, taking the accepted ideas and doing little to criticize or analyze them. To Shaw, this was indefensible. Shakespeare's creative effort should have been directed to standing those accepted ideas on their heads, as Shaw was doing with the accepted ideas of the late nineteenth century.

Can Shaw's charge against Shakespeare be turned against himself? Is Shaw really any more of an original thinker than Shakespeare? Again it depends on the definition of original thinker. Not surprisingly, Shaw is more original as defined by Shaw: the tester of creeds and codes. That is surely not Shakespeare's specialty. But by the usual definition of a man concocting his own ideas, Shaw the crow following many ploughs is not original. Both playwrights were remarkable assimilators of other men's ideas. Shakespeare assimilated the accepted ideas; Shaw assimilated the avant-garde. And even Shakespeare took ideas from the avant-garde, Montaigne, for example.

Shaw also reproached Shakespeare for pessimism. That is not an allowable objection to Shakespeare or any other author. Optimism or pessimism *per se* is not the important thing, as Harold Clurman says:

> It does not matter in art whether or not one is a pessimist or an optimist. To say that life is lovely is no more correct, convincing, moving or significant than to say it is horrid. It is the substance—not the conclusion—of an argument that gives it validity. Its *living matter*—the images, forms, characters, incidents, evocation of experience, life-content—give a work of art its power, meaning and value. If these are rich, then the work is creative no matter how white or black the summation of the whole may be.[9]

The living matter in both Shakespeare and Shaw is what keeps them readable and playable, not their degree of pessimism or optimism, originality or familiarity of thought. In his distinction between writers of the first and second order, Shaw assumed that the conclusion, not the substance, of the argument counted for practically everything. If an author rejected his time, then Shaw was on his side. If an author accepted his time, then Shaw was on his back. This simpleminded approach led him into some peculiar opinions, like his preference for the playwright Brieux. The conclusion of Brieux's argument proved that his heart was in the right place. The substance of Brieux's argument was mediocre at best.

If, as Clurman says, the substance rather than the conclusion of an argument gives it validity, then Shaw's distinction between writers of the first and second order is beside the point. Shaw thought that the substance of his own plays—character and plot—was subordinate to the conclusion —the attacks on accepted ideas. But those attacks, once so conspicuous, no longer surprise or dismay. They are givens. The substance, however, remains to delight. Shaw was too good a playwright to adhere to his own standards for playwriting. If he had been less skillful with characters and plot, he might now be vaguely remembered as that interesting fellow, Mr. Shaw, who rattled off ideas some years ago, and whatever happened to him anyway? Shaw cannot be taken at his own evaluation. As he describes them, his best plays often sound like awful bores, earnest specimens of social consciousness. Shaw the thinker was not so brilliant as Shaw the artist.

Although Shaw insists on his originality as a tester of creeds and codes, he denies the originality of his dramatic technique. In an article, "A Dramatic Realist to His Critics" (1894), Shaw says about *Arms and the Man:* "I am, among other things, a dramatist; but I am not an original one, and so have to take all my dramatic material either from real life at first hand, or from authentic documents."[10] An original dramatist might start from scratch. Shaw does not. From the evidence of life and documents, the military is outrageous. *Arms and the Man* shows it up. Shaw does not construct gossamer fantasies without point or connection to actual conditions.

In "Better than Shakespear?" Shaw gave another reason for his unoriginal technique; he filched, not only from life and documents, but also from other playwrights:

Technically, I do not find myself able to proceed otherwise than as former playwrights have done. True, my plays have the latest mechanical improvements: the action is not carried on by impossible soliloquys and asides; and my people get on and off the stage without requiring four doors to a room which in real life would have only one. But my stories are the old stories; my characters are the familiar harlequin and columbine, clown and pantaloon (note the harlequin's leap in the third act of Caesar and Cleopatra) ; my stage tricks and suspenses and thrills and jests are the ones in vogue when I was a boy, by which time my grandfather was tired of them.[11]

That is a warning not to separate Shaw from the longstanding theatrical conventions. Shaw knew all the tricks of the trade very well. This is also an implied warning for those who find Shaw a realist in form. Harlequin and columbine, clown and pantaloon would not be appropriate in the work of a realist. Shaw wanted to persuade his audiences that certain views were correct, but he never underestimated the importance of keeping them amused. Shaw hoped that they would remember socialism and the life force as well as the clown. He asserts that the ideas in *Caesar and Cleopatra* are distinctively modern and non-Shakespearean. Yet when it comes to projecting those ideas, Shaw falls back on the time-honored devices. The content may not be familiar, but the form is.

Shaw repeated his denial of technical originality in an article, "What is the Finest Dramatic Situation?" He complains that audiences cannot distinguish the new from the old:

I am constantly praised—as all our leading playwrights are praised—for old professional tricks that we do no better than Robertson or Charles Reade, or Tom Taylor or Bulwer Lytton, or Plautus or Terence; whilst the real advances we make are either missed altogether or complained of as "undramatic," or some such nonsense.[12]

This statement has a tinge of unionism, as a carpenter would modestly claim that his own efforts were no more than what his fellow-craftsmen had done. Insignificant playwrights like Bulwer Lytton get credit for the old professional tricks.

Plautus and Terence fall naturally into the succession of superior playwrights, but the other four are ill at ease in the company of Shaw (although he is at home in theirs). But that is Shaw's point. The worst and best writers dip into the same bag of tricks, while the really original points are missed or misunderstood. He is referring to the opinion, widely held at the time, that his plays are not dramatic at all but excuses for an exhibition of Hyde Park oratory. Shaw was more than justified in calling such an idea nonsense.

In the preface to *Back to Methuselah*, Shaw says again that his technique is traditional:

> People talked as if there had been no dramatic or descriptive music before Wagner; no impressionist painting before Whistler; whilst as to myself, I was finding that the surest way to produce an effect of daring innovation and originality was to revive the ancient attraction of long rhetorical speeches; to stick closely to the methods of Molière; and to lift characters bodily out of the pages of Charles Dickens.[13]

Shaw is an assimilator and thief. Long rhetorical speeches were an old theatrical device, but people did not expect to find them in contemporary drama, particularly in comedies. Do people in drawing rooms make long, modulated speeches? Of course not, but then Shaw was not trying to give an accurate slice of drawing-room life.

His comment about Dickens is suggestive. Shaw may not have lifted bodily, but some of his characters are Dickensian. The charlatans in *The Doctor's Dilemma* owe as much to Dickens as to Molière.[14] They are droll and dotty, a line-up of Dickens eccentrics.

Shaw made this sensible evaluation of his plays:

> If you want to flatter me you must not tell me that I have saved your soul by my philosophy. Tell me that, like Shakespear, Molière, Scott, Dumas, and Dickens, I have provided a gallery of characters which are realer to you than your own

relations and which successive generations of actors and actresses will keep alive for centuries as their *chevaux de bataille*.[15]

Shaw's plays are centripetal, the ideas whirling in toward the characters at the core.

Shaw went even further in asserting that he was a traditional author. In fact, his methods and Shakespeare's were not so different after all:

> Neither have I ever been what you call a representationist or realist. I was always in the classic tradition, recognizing that stage characters must be endowed by the author with a conscious self-knowledge and power of expression, and, as you observe with genuine penetration, a freedom from inhibitions, which in real life would make them monsters of genius. It is the power to do this that differentiates me (or Shakespear) from a gramophone and a camera.[16]

Attempts to tag Shaw as a realist in form are futile. Nobody could really be as brilliant and charming as the characters in his plays. As he suggests, that is probably a good thing. Such people would be nothing less than overwhelming. Real people, Shaw implies, do not have "conscious self-knowledge and power of expression." Art ought to improve on life instead of copying it.

In reviewing *My Fair Lady*, Harold Clurman said that Shaw never was a realist:

> Shaw is Punch and Judy, vaudeville and rhetoric informed by paradoxical common sense and joyous wisdom. His speeches are comic tirades (consider Doolittle's contrast of lower-class morality with that of the wealthy) or virtuoso arias in the grand manner—full of humanitarian passion and robust conviction. Shaw's quips, gags, handsprings and somersaults derive from the oldest of old theatre—which is one reason they endure. Shaw's lineage is the "classic" theatre from the street harlequinade to grand opera. That is why he seems very much himself in the new framework.[17]

This review demonstrates the special advantage of the theater reviewer. From observing actual productions, he is led to a further understanding of the play. Play and production clarify each other. The theater reviewer is not in business just to comment on actors, sets, and wigs. The final goal should be intelligent comment on the most important thing—the text.

Shaw often emphasized the influence of music in constructing his plays:

> Again you are right when you say that my technique is classic and Molièresque (the *Commedia dell'Arte* was improvised Molière). Your word "kinship," too, to express the relation between me and Congreve and Sheridan is precisely correct. We are all three Irishmen: that is all. They had no part whatever in forming my habits. On the other hand, the fact that I was brought up on Italian and German opera must have influenced me a great deal: there is much more of Il Trovatore and Don Giovanni in my style than of The Mourning Bride and The School for Scandal; but it would take me too far to pursue this.[18]

Unfortunately Shaw did not pursue his indebtedness to Verdi and Mozart. Even the most cogent explanations of how music is transmuted into literature are not totally persuasive. It is chemistry subtle almost to the point of impossibility, like converting silver to platinum. As for Shaw and Mozart, *Man and Superman* and *Don Giovanni* come first to mind. Shaw took many themes and ideas from the opera, but is the influence Mozart's music or Da Ponte's libretto? Shaw's speeches are arias of sorts. His ensembles have the qualities of Mozart opera, where several voices interweave in a way that is both dramatically apt and appealing to the ear. "Rhetorical" has become a term of abuse. This is unfortunate. Shaw is the most rhetorical of writers, that is, he indulges in musical overstatement. At his best, Shaw exerts optimum self-control over his characters' extravagance of language. Shaw's dramatic language is always very much his own; it is also the language of a particular character. Zerlina and Donna Anna both sound like Mozart, but they also sound like themselves.

Shortly before his death, Shaw repeated that opera helped him in organizing his plays:

> Opera taught me to shape my plays into recitatives, arias, duets, trios, ensemble finales, and bravura pieces to display the technical accomplishments of the executants, with the quaint result that all the critics, friendly and hostile, took my plays to be so new, so extraordinary, so revolutionary, that the Times critic declared they were not plays at all as plays had been defined for all time by Aristotle.[19]

The *Times* critic was A. B. Walkley. Confronted with a new Shaw play, he sang the same refrain: it is not a drama. This cant is based on the assumption that somewhere an entity, "drama pure and simple," floats in the empyrean. Max Beerbohm had to swallow his own words about the dramatic quality in Shaw. He first reviewed the published *Man and Superman,* then saw it on the stage and changed his mind:

> I myself was rash enough to prophesy that "Man and Superman," though I had delighted in reading it, would be quite ineffective on the stage. I still blush when I remember that pronouncement; and caution strongly inclines me to take any new work of Mr. Shaw's at whatever valuation he may set on it.[20]

Reviewers who found Shaw undramatic could not recognize vitality under their noses. And, Shaw complained, they did not spot the old theatrical tricks. What was original about rhetoric and word music? The reviewers were tone-deaf. Such graceful and musical dialogue had not been heard on the English stage since Sheridan, except for Wilde.

Poetic justice might be served if a playwright-propagandist, after listening to Shaw's recitatives and arias, should say,

"This Shaw fellow is no thinker at all but a word-musician."
The ghost of Shakespeare would surely smile. Shaw never
denied that his plays were musical compositions; he pro-
claimed his resemblances to Mozart and Verdi. (He would
have bristled at the idea that his plays were *primarily*
musical compositions.) Shaw did have a fine ear, and his
plays have a distinguishable ring and melody. T. S. Eliot
has thus described Shaw's dramatic prose:

> Our two greatest prose stylists in the drama—apart from
> Shakespeare and the other Elizabethans who mixed prose and
> verse in the same play—are, I believe, Congreve and Bernard
> Shaw. A speech by a character of Congreve or of Shaw has—
> however clearly the characters may be differentiated—that un-
> mistakable personal rhythm which is the mark of a prose style,
> and of which only the most accomplished conversationalists—
> who are for that matter usually monologuists—show any trace
> in their talk. We have all heard (too often) of Molière's
> character who expressed surprise when told he spoke prose.
> But it was Mr. Jourdain who was right, and not his mentor
> or his creator: he did not speak prose—he only talked. For
> I mean to draw a triple distinction; between prose, and verse,
> and our ordinary speech which is mostly below the level of
> either verse or prose. So if you look at it in this way, it will
> appear that prose, on the stage, is as artificial as verse: or
> alternatively, that verse can be as natural as prose.[21]

Eliot is propagandist for his verse dramas. His paradox
makes sense. Shaw's prose, artificial as verse, is above the
level of ordinary speech. If a person entered a room and
heard conversation like Shaw's, he could count it an ex-
ceptional day.

Shaw was asked to explain his principles as a playwright.
He made a characteristic snort of a reply: "I am not governed
by principles; I am inspired, how or why I cannot explain,
because I do not know; but inspiration it must be; for
it comes to me without any reference to my own ends or
interest."[22] Then he mentions the factors not directly connected with the muses:

I have to think of my pocket, of the manager's pocket, of the actors' pockets, of the spectators' pockets, of how long people can be kept sitting in a theatre without relief or refreshments, of the range of the performer's voice, and of the hearing and vision of the boy at the back of the gallery, whose right to be put in full possession of the play is as sacred as that of the millionaire in the stalls or boxes.

This is inspiration with both feet on the ground.

Shaw rejected dramatic principles, because they could easily turn into formulas. He relates an argument with William Archer about the French theater of the nineteenth century. Archer liked it; Shaw did not:

> I held, on the contrary, that a play is a vital growth and not a mechanical construction; that a plot is the ruin of a story and therefore of a play, which is essentially a story; that Shakespear's plays and Dickens's novels, though redeemed by their authors' genius, were as ridiculous in their plots as Goldsmith's hopelessly spoilt Goodnatured Man: in short, that a play should never have a plot, because, if it has any natural life in it, it will construct itself, like a flowering plant, far more wonderfully than its author can consciously construct it.[23]

Despite Shaw's assertion to the contrary, his plays are well constructed. In *Pygmalion*, each act proceeds in a logical and lively step. The last four acts alternate between Higgins's house and his mother's. But the structure is not obtrusive; the vital growth is much in evidence.

Archer put his finger on a peculiarity of nineteenth-century theater reviewing:

> The great critics of the past, so far as they dealt with the theatre of their own time, were critics, not of drama, but of acting. Who remembers a single thing that Lamb, or Hazlitt, or Leigh Hunt, or John Forster, or George Henry Lewes, ever said of a contemporary play?[24]

Hazlitt wrote about Edmund Kean, Shaw about Henry

Irving. Hazlitt expanded his criticism of acting to talk about Shakespeare in general. So did Shaw, but with an important twist. Shakespeare was the means, not the end. He was only a stepping stone; Ibsen and Shaw waited at the other side of the stream. Hazlitt had no contemporary writer of stature to champion, nor was he a playwright. He could afford to be an objective critic of Shakespeare. For Shaw, the new drama was at hand, and audiences had to realize it. He may be forgiven for berating the old chestnuts, even if Shakespeare was *the* chestnut of them all.

The air of the English theater had been still far too long. Whirlwinds, not breezes, were required to change it. If the public, by force of habit, preferred Shakespeare, then Shakespeare had to give way. "A tower of the Bastille," Shaw called him. He was stronger than that, as Shaw well knew. He did not really expect Ibsen and Shaw to replace Shakespeare, but he did want the moderns to receive their due alongside him. Driving the public into the Ibsen whirlwind, he stirred up his own. A lesser man would only have created a disturbance. Shaw both heralded and created a drama.

Notes

The books cited most often are the three volumes of *Our Theatres in the Nineties* (abbreviated as *OTN*) in the Standard Edition (London, 1954); the collected *Prefaces* (London, 1934); and *Shaw on Theatre,* ed. E. J. West (New York, 1958). As far as possible I have taken other quotations from the Ayot St. Lawrence Edition of *The Collected Works of Bernard Shaw* (referred to in the notes as *Works*), 30 vols. (New York, 1930–32). The date of each review in *Our Theatres in the Nineties* is included, because there are other editions.

1
Introduction

1. Preface to *Three Plays for Puritans, Prefaces,* p. 706.
2. *OTN,* 3:385 (21 May 1898)

2
Putting Shakespeare to Use

1. *Works,* 1: xii.
2. "The Invective of Henry Arthur Jones" (*The Sunday Chronicle,* 20 November 1921), an article by Shaw, is part of his book, *Pen Portraits and Reviews,* in *Works,* 29:188.
3. *George Bernard Shaw, His Life and Personality* (New York, 1963), p. 15.
4. *OTN,* 2:196 (26 September 1896).
5. In Raymond Mander and Joe Mitchenson, *Theatrical Companion to Shaw* (London, 1954), p. 273.
6. *Prefaces,* p. 56.
7. *OTN,* 2:110 (2 May 1896).
8. *Theatrical Companion,* p. 273.
9. *Works,* 30:265.
10. *Prefaces,* p. 555.
11. *Works,* 20:52.
12. *Sixteen Self Sketches* (New York, 1949), p. 152.
13. *Bernard Shaw's Letters to Granville Barker,* ed. C. B. Purdom (New York, 1957), p. 199 (14 September 1943).
14. *Bernard Shaw and Mrs. Patrick Campbell: Their Correspondence,* ed. Alan Dent (London, 1952), p. 110 (22 April 1913).

15. *Short Stories, Scraps, and Shavings,* in *Works,* 6:77.
16. *Ibid.*
17. *Ibid.* p. 79.
18. "Mr Arnold Bennett Thinks Playwriting Easier Than Novel Writing," *The Nation,* 11 March 1916; from *Pen Portraits and Reviews,* in *Works,* 29:46ff.
19. *Works,* 15:203.
20. *Works,* 17:198.
21. *Geneva, Cymbeline Refinished, & Good King Charles* (London, 1946), p. 171.
22. *Ibid.,* p. 203.
23. *Works,* 12:169.
24. *Works,* 15:59–60.
25. *Ibid.,* p. 135.
26. *Works,* 16:47.
27. *Ibid.,* p. 184.
28. *Works,* 13:238.
29. *Ibid.,* p. 243.
30. *Ibid.,* p. 249.
31. "The National Shakespear Theatre and the New Repertory Theatres," *The Times,* 10 May 1909.
32. Preface to *Heartbreak House, Prefaces,* p. 393.
33. Program from the National Theatre.
34. *Buoyant Billions, Farfetched Fables, & Shakes Versus Shav* (London, 1950), p. 140.
35. *Ibid.,* p. 141.
36. *Ibid.,* p. 143.
37. *Prefaces,* p. 724.
38. *Ibid.,* p. 739.
39. *Translations and Tomfooleries,* in *Works,* 18:93.
40. *Ibid.,* p. 112.
41. *Ibid.,* p. 125.
42. *Geneva, Cymbeline Refinished, & Good King Charles,* p. 137.
43. *Ibid.,* p. 136.
44. *Ibid.,* p. 142.
45. *Ibid.,* p. 148.
46. *Ibid.*
47. *Prefaces,* p. 593.
48. *Correspondence,* p. 147 (8 September 1913).
49. *OTN,* 3:1–8 (2 January 1897).
50. *Prefaces,* p. 718.
51. *Ibid.,* p. 720.
52. *Sixteen Self Sketches,* p. 153.

53. *Music in London, Works,* 26–28; 27:315 (3 May 1893).
54. J. P. Eckermann, *Conversations with Goethe,* trans. John Oxenford, ed. J. K. Moorhead (London and New York, 1951), p. 32.
55. Shaw, *Collected Letters 1898–1910,* ed. Dan H. Laurence (New York, 1972).

3
Shaw's Principles of Criticism
1. *Curtains* (New York, 1961), p. 295.
2. *OTN,* 1:v.
3. *Lies Like Truth* (New York, 1960), p. 140.
4. *How to Become a Musical Critic,* ed. Dan H. Laurence (London, 1960), p. 265 (2 April 1910).
5. *OTN,* 1:130 (25 May 1895).
6. *The Playwright as Thinker* (New York, 1946), p. 142.
7. *Table-Talk of G.B.S.,* ed. Archibald Henderson (New York, 1925), p. 44.
8. *Music in London,* in *Works,* 28:146 (24 January 1894).
9. *Prefaces,* p. 717.
10. *Ibid.,* p. 711.
11. *The Perfect Wagnerite,* in *Works,* 19:191.
12. *Ibid.,* p. 231.
13. *Ibid.,* p. 247.
14. *Music in London,* in *Works,* 27:302 (19 April 1893).
15. *The Mikado and Five Other Savoy Operas* (New York, 1961), p. 301.
16. *Prefaces,* p. 434.
17. *Ibid.,* p. 419.
18. *Ibid.,* p. 436.
19. *Ibid.,* p. 112.
20. *Ibid.,* p. 228.
21. Letter to Alan S. Downer, 21 January 1948, in Martin Meisel, *Shaw and the Nineteenth-Century Theater* (Princeton, 1963), p. 92.
22. *Prefaces,* p. 204.
23. *Buoyant Billions, Farfetched Fables, & Shakes Versus Shav,* p. 65.
24. *Ibid.*
25. "The Artstruck Englishman," *The Nation,* 17 February 1917; from *Pen Portraits and Reviews,* in *Works,* 29:244.
26. *George Bernard Shaw: A Critical Survey,* ed. Louis Kronenberger (Cleveland and New York, 1953), p. 131; also in Wilson's *The Triple Thinkers* (New York, 1948), p. 171.
27. *Music in London,* in *Works,* 26:54 (30 September 1890).

28. *OTN*, 2:233 (31 October 1896).
29. Introduction to *The Critic and the Drama* (New York, 1922).
30. *Music in London*, in *Works*, 28:249 (13 June 1894).
31. *Comedians All* (New York, 1919), p. 203.
32. *Music in London*, in *Works*, 27:338 (31 May 1893).
33. *OTN*, 1:65 (16 March 1895).
34. *Ibid.*, 2:85 (4 April 1896).
35. In S. N. Behrman, *Portrait of Max* (New York, 1960), p. 166.
36. *Around Theatres*, 2 vols. (New York, 1930), 1:12 (1 October 1898).
37. *Ibid.*, p. 56 (18 November 1899).
38. *OTN*, 2:140 (30 May 1896).
39. *Ibid.*, 1:248 (16 November 1895).
40. *Music in London*, in *Works*, 27:21 (3 February 1892).
41. *Prefaces*, p. 712.
42. *Ibid.*, p. 713.
43. "George Bernard Shaw," *Fortnightly Review* (August 1931).
44. *OTN*, 1:vii.

4
Music and Thought: Shakespeare vs. Ibsen

1. *Sixteen Self Sketches*, p. 200.
2. *The Quintessence of Ibsenism*, in *Works*, 19:152.
3. *Ibid.*, p. 155.
4. *OTN*, 1:27 (2 February 1895).
5. *Ibid.*, 3:209 (9 October 1897).
6. *The Quintessence of Ibsenism*, in *Works*, 19:53.
7. *Shaw on Theatre*, ed. E. J. West (New York, 1958), p. 63.
8. *OTN*, 3:141 (22 May 1897).
9. *Works*, 7:68–147.
10. *Ibid.*, p. 88.
11. *Ibid.*, p. 111.
12. *OTN*, 3:344 (26 March 1898).
13. Preface to *The Admirable Bashville*, *Prefaces*, p. 741.
14. *GBS, His Life and Personality*, p. 459.
15. *Prefaces*, p. 201.
16. *Ibid.*, p. 522.
17. Shaw, *Collected Letters 1898–1910*, p. 802.
18. *Shaw on Theatre*, p. 218.
19. *Ibid.*, p. 220
20. "The New York Times, Alas, Alas," *Esquire* (May 1963), p. 144.
21. *London Music* (London, 1950), p. 82 (23 March 1889).
22. *OTN*, 1:24–30 (2 February 1895).

23. *London Music,* p. 285 (10 January 1890).
24. *Ellen Terry and Bernard Shaw: A Correspondence,* ed. Christopher St. John (New York, 1931), p. 33 (28 August 1896).
25. *Bernard Shaw and Mrs. Patrick Campbell: Their Correspondence,* p. 218 (13 January 1921).
26. *OTN,* 2:130 (16 May 1896).
27. *Ibid.,* 3:301 (29 January 1898).
28. *Music in London,* in *Works,* 28:140 (17 January 1894).
29. "The Author's Apology" to *Mrs Warren's Profession, Prefaces,* p. 227.
30. *Shaw on Theatre,* p. 123.
31. *OTN,* 3:323 (26 February 1898).
32. *Ibid.,* pp. 76–83 (20 March 1897).
33. *Ibid.,* p. 134 (15 May 1897).
34. *Ibid.,* p. 146 (29 May 1897).
35. *George Bernard Shaw* (New York, 1962), p. 72.
36. *Ibid.*
37. "A Word More About Verdi," *The Anglo-Saxon Review* (March 1901); in *London Music,* p. 413.
38. *Short Stories, Scraps, and Shavings,* in *Works,* 6:85–91.
39. *Prefaces,* p. 40.
40. *The Quintessence of Ibsenism,* in *Works,* 19:151.
41. *OTN,* 3:147 (29 May 1897).
42. *Ibid.,* p. 148.
43. In *GBS, His Life and Personality,* p. 224.
44. *The Quintessence of Ibsenism,* in *Works,* 19:152.
45. *Table-Talk of G.B.S.,* p. 40.
46. In Archibald Henderson, *Bernard Shaw, Playboy and Prophet* (New York, 1932), p. 336.
47. *Prefaces,* p. 155.
48. *OTN,* 2:82 (28 March 1896).
49. *Works,* 5:270.
50. Preface to *Plays Unpleasant, Prefaces,* p. 692.
51. MS Eng 1046.1 in Harvard College Library.
52. MS Thr 35.1 in Harvard College Library.
53. *Prefaces,* p. 162.
54. *Ibid.,* p. 163.
55. *Works,* 2:xix; also *Prefaces,* p. 656.

5
Shakespearean Production

1. In order of presentation: *Hamlet, The Merchant of Venice, Othello, Romeo and Juliet, Much Ado About Nothing, Twelfth*

Night, Macbeth, Henry VIII, King Lear, Cymbeline, Richard III, and *Coriolanus.*
2. *The London News,* 26 September 1896.
3. Print Room, Victoria and Albert Museum, Box 94.G.26.
4. The Folger Shakespeare Library, Prompt Ham. 20.
5. Print Room, Victoria and Albert Museum, Box D.T.43.
6. *Ibid.,* Box D.T.44.
7. John Coleman, *Memoirs of Samuel Phelps* (London, 1886), p. 217.
8. *The Architectural Review,* July 1901.
9. *Romeo and Juliet as Arranged for the Stage by Forbes Robertson* (London, 1895).
10. *Dramatic Values* (New York, 1911), p. 202.
11. *A Player Under Three Reigns* (London, 1925), after p. 116.
12. (Leipzig, n.d.), p. 170.
13. *Souvenir of King Henry VIII at the Lyceum* (London, 1892).
14. Print Room, Victoria and Albert Museum, Box D.T. 29e.
15. *The Architectural Review,* July 1898.
16. *Ibid.,* November 1900.
17. In the Harvard Theatre Collection.
18. Starring Richard Burton, Eileen Herlie, and Hume Cronyn.
19. *Thoughts and After-Thoughts* (London, 1913), p. 52.
20. George C. D. Odell, *Shakespeare—From Betterton to Irving,* 2 vols. (New York, 1963), 2:413.
21. *Prefaces,* p. 776.
22. *Henry Irving* (New York, 1930), p. 139.
23. *A Life in the Theatre* (New York, 1959), p. 120.
24. In Laurence Irving, *Henry Irving: The Actor and His World* (London, 1951), p. 535.
25. *London Music,* p. 94 (5 April 1889).
26. *OTN,* 3:185 (10 July 1897).
27. *Around Theatres,* 2:512 (21 October 1905).
28. In *GBS, His Life and Personality,* p. 158.
29. *Prefaces,* p. 758.
30. *Correspondence,* p. 43 (8 September 1896).
31. In the Enthoven Collection, Victoria and Albert Museum.
32. *Prefaces,* p. 753.
33. *Ibid.,* p. 754.
34. *The Theatrical 'World' of 1896* (London, 1897), p. 345.
35. *Henry Irving, Actor and Manager* (London, 1883), p. 47.
36. *Ellen Terry's Memoirs,* ed. Edith Craig and Christopher St. John (New York, 1932), p. 82.
37. "The Fashionable Tragedian," first ed. (Edinburgh, 1877), p. 5.

38. "A Letter Concerning Mr. Henry Irving" (Edinburgh, 1877), p. 6.
39. "The Fashionable Tragedian," 2d ed. (London, 1877), p. 26.
40. *Ellen Terry's Memoirs*, p. 57.
41. *Ibid.*, p. 215.
42. *Henry Irving, Actor and Manager*, p. 77.
43. *OTN*, 2:198 (26 September 1896).
44. "The Actor-Manager and the Playwright," *Harper's Bazar* (November 1920).
45. *OTN*, 1:12 (19 January 1895).
46. *Ibid.*, 3:39 (6 February 1897).
47. *Henry Irving*, p. 191.
48. *OTN*, 2:199 (26 September 1896).
49. Letter to the Editor, *The Standard*, 30 October 1905.
50. *Correspondence*, p. 59 (23 September 1896).
51. *OTN*, 2:195 (26 September 1896).
52. *The Scenic Art*, ed. Allan Wade (New Brunswick, N.J., 1948), p. 282.
53. *Ibid.*, p. 139.
54. *The Drama* (Boston, 1892), p. 21.
55. *The Literary Digest*, 14 November 1896.
56. In *GBS, His Life and Personality*, p. 161.
57. *Pen Portraits and Reviews*, in *Works*, 29:171.
58. Preface to *Plays Unpleasant, Prefaces*, p. 691.
59. *King Lear as Arranged for the Stage by Henry Irving* (London, 1893), p. 5.
60. *Shakespeare—From Betterton to Irving*, 2:352.
61. *Souvenir of King Lear at the Lyceum* (London, 1892).
62. *King Lear at the Lyceum. Some Extracts from the Press* (London, 1893), p. 116.
63. *Shakespearean Playgoing, 1890–1952* (London, 1953), p. 12.
64. *From "The Bells" to "King Arthur"* (London, 1897), p. 349.
65. *Shakespeare in the Theatre* (London, 1913), p. 186.
66. Robert Speaight, *William Poel and the Elizabethan Revival* (Cambridge, Mass., 1954), p. 228.
67. The Folger Shakespeare Library, Prompt Mu. Ad. 8.
68. *OTN*, 3:325 (26 February 1898).
69. The Folger Shakespeare Library, Prompt Cor. 7.
70. *Irving's King Lear*, p. 5.
71. *Ibid.*, p. 14.
72. *Ibid.*, p. 15.
73. *Shaw on Theatre*, p. 45.
74. *OTN*, 2:197 (26 September 1896).

75. "Shakespeare as a Playwright," *The Works of William Shakespeare,* ed. Sir Henry Irving and Frank A. Marshall (London, 1888), 1:xxi.
76. *Music in London,* in *Works,* 27:15 (27 January 1892).
77. *OTN,* 2:159–65 (20 June 1896).
78. Courtesy of the Canadian Broadcasting Company.
79. *Shaw on Theatre,* p. 183.
80. *William Poel and the Elizabethan Revival,* p. 50.
81. *Ibid.,* p. 72.
82. *Ibid.,* p. 90.
83. *Ibid.,* p. 32.
84. *Monthly Letters,* ed. A. M. T[rethewy] (London, 1929), p. 3.
85. *Shaw on Theatre,* p. 136.
86. *William Poel and the Elizabethan Revival,* p. 151.
87. *Ibid.,* p. 100.
88. *London Music,* p. 322 (28 February 1890).
89. "London Shakespeare League: Report of a public discussion on the best method of presenting Shakespeare's plays" (London, 1905), p. 9.
90. *OTN,* 1:190 (20 July 1895).
91. *Ibid.,* p. 189.
92. *Ibid.,* 3:193 (17 July 1897).
93. *Ibid.,* p. 242 (13 November 1897).
94. *The Theatrical 'World' of 1897* (London, 1898), p. 315.
95. *OTN,* 3:243 (13 November 1897).
96. *Ibid.*
97. In Joseph Harker, *Studio and Stage* (London, 1924), p. 188.
98. *Ibid.,* p. 187.
99. *The Theatrical 'World' of 1895* (London, 1896), p. 220.
100. *Drama and Life* (London, 1907), p. 137.
101. *Around Theatres,* 1:331 (20 June 1903).
102. *Dramatic Values,* p. 244.
103. *William Poel and the Elizabethan Revival,* p. 246.
104. *OTN,* 2:185.
105. *The Dramatic Review* (19 September 1885).
106. In order of frequency of performance: *Man and Superman, You Never Can Tell, John Bull's Other Island, The Admirable Bashville, Major Barbara, The Doctor's Dilemma, Candida, How He Lied to Her Husband, The Philanderer, Don Juan in Hell,* and *The Man of Destiny.* (*Theatrical Companion,* p. 287).
107. Preface to the 4th ed. of *The Perfect Wagnerite* (1922), in *Works,* 19:167.
108. *Harley Granville Barker* (London, 1955), p. 169.

109. *Correspondence*, p. 173 (27 July 1897).
110. *Harley Granville Barker*, p. 41.
111. *The Last Actor-Managers* (London, 1950), p. 73.
112. *Shaw on Theatre*, p. 266.
113. *Ibid.*, p. 267.
114. "Hints on Rehearsing a Play." MS in the British Theatre Museum Association. Quoted by permission of the Garrick Club.
115. *Theatrical Companion*, p. 18.
116. *Bernard Shaw, Director* (Seattle, 1971), p. 13.
117. *Ibid.*, p. 65.
118. *Advice to a Young Critic*, ed. E. J. West (New York, 1955), p. 62 (26 September 1896).
119. *London Music*, p. 356 (18 April 1890).
120. *Shaw on Theatre*, p. 158.
121. *Prefaces*, p. 776.
122. *Lies Like Truth*, p. 140.
123. *Shaw on Theatre*, p. 284; also *Theatrical Companion*, p. 9.
124. *Shaw on Theatre*, p. 82.
125. *Ibid.*, p. 284; also *Theatrical Companion*, p. 9.
126. In W. J. Lawrence, *Barry Sullivan: A Biographical Sketch* (London, 1893), p. 18.
127. *Shaw on Theatre*, p. 270.
128. *OTN*, 1:271 (14 December 1895).
129. *Shaw on Theatre*, p. 274.
130. Preface to *The Dark Lady of the Sonnets*, *Prefaces*, p. 735.
131. *OTN*, 1:272 (14 December 1895).
132. "The Religion of the Pianoforte," *The Fortnightly Review* (February 1894); in *How to Become a Musical Critic*, p. 214.
133. *OTN*, 1:183 (13 July 1895).
134. *Prefaces*, p. 751.
135. *OTN*, 1:273 (14 December 1895).
136. *Prefaces*, p. 751.
137. *OTN*, 1:177–84 (13 July 1895).
138. *Ibid.*, p. 167 (29 June 1895).
139. *Pen Portraits and Reviews*, in *Works*, 29:290.
140. *Beerbohm Tree, His Life and Laughter* (London, 1956), p. 130.
141. *Shaw on Theatre*, p. 96.
142. *Correspondence*, p. 15 (1 November 1895).
143. *Correspondence*, p. 216 (22 December 1920).
144. *OTN*, 3:200 (2 October 1897).
145. *Shakespearean Playgoing*, p. 46.
146. *Some Notable "Hamlets" of the Present Time* (London, 1905), p. 137.

147. *The Theatrical 'World' of 1897*, p. 255.
148. *OTN*, 3:201 (2 October 1897).
149. *Theatrical Companion*, p. 63.
150. *OTN*, 3:206 (2 October 1897).
151. *Correspondence*, p. 59 (23 September 1896).
152. *OTN*, 3:270 (18 December 1897).
153. "Shakespearean Recital," two 78 rpm records, D4006 and D4007, Columbia Gramophone Co. (1928); courtesy of Professor Frederick C. Packard, Jr., of Harvard.
154. Letter to Alan S. Downer, 12 November 1947, in *Shaw and the Nineteenth-Century Theater*, p. 98.
155. *Shaw on Theatre*, pp. 166–69.
156. *William Poel and the Elizabethan Revival*, p. 28.

6
The Exposer Exposed

1. *OTN*, 3:210 (9 October 1897).
2. "Shaw as Drama Critic," *Theatre Arts* (May 1951), p. 95.
3. *The Quintessence of Ibsenism*, in *Works*, 19:32.
4. *Ibid.*, p. 34.
5. *Ibid.*, p. 45.
6. *Ibid.*, p. 157.
7. *Works*, 20:375.
8. *Prefaces*, p. 721.
9. *Lies Like Truth*, p. 85.
10. *Shaw on Theatre*, p. 19.
11. *Prefaces*, p. 720.
12. *Shaw on Theatre*, p. 111.
13. *Prefaces*, p. 479.
14. *Works*, 12:1–179.
15. *Shaw on Theatre*, p. 242.
16. *Ibid.*, p. 185.
17. *Lies Like Truth*, p. 116.
18. *Shaw on Theatre*, p. 185.
19. *Ibid.*, p. 294.
20. *Around Theatres*, 2:656 (23 May 1908).
21. "Poetry and Drama," *On Poetry and Poets* (London, 1957), p. 73.
22. *Shaw on Theatre*, p. 116.
23. "How William Archer Impressed Bernard Shaw," Shaw's Foreword to Archer's *Three Plays* (1927), from *Pen Portraits and Reviews*, in *Works*, 29:23.
24. *The Old Drama and the New* (Boston, 1923), p. 114.

Bibliography

By Shaw

"The Actor-Manager and the Playwright." *Harper's Bazar*, November 1920.

Advice to a Young Critic. Edited by E. J. West. New York, 1955.

Arms and the Man. Typescript, 1894, with revisions in Shaw's hand. MS Eng 1046.1. Harvard College Library.

Berg Collection. New York Public Library. Manuscripts.

Bernard Shaw and Mrs. Patrick Campbell: Their Correspondence. Edited by Alan Dent. London, 1952.

Bernard Shaw's Letters to Granville Barker. Edited by C. B. Purdom. New York, 1957.

British Museum. Add. MSS. 50508–50743.

Buoyant Billions, Farfetched Fables, & Shakes Versus Shav. London, 1950.

Collected Letters 1898–1910. Edited by Dan H. Laurence. New York, 1972.

The Collected Works of Bernard Shaw. Ayot St. Lawrence ed. 30 vols. New York, 1930–32.

Ellen Terry and Bernard Shaw: A Correspondence. Edited by Christopher St. John. New York, 1931.

Geneva, Cymbeline Refinished, & Good King Charles. London, 1946.

How to Become a Musical Critic. Edited by Dan H. Laurence. London, 1960.

London Music. London, 1950.

Major Barbara. Typescript with notations, 1905, used as prompt copy for Royal Court Theatre. MS Thr 35.1. Harvard College Library.

"The National Shakespear Theatre and the New Repertory Theatres." *The Times,* 10 May 1909.

Our Theatres in the Nineties. Standard ed. 3 vols. London, 1954.

Prefaces. London, 1934.

"Qualifications of the Complete Actor." *The Dramatic Review*, 19 September 1885.

Shaw collection of Beinecke Library, Yale University. Newspaper and magazine articles.

Shaw on Music. Edited by Eric Bentley. New York, 1955.

Shaw on Shakespeare. Edited by Edwin Wilson. New York, 1961.

Shaw on Theatre. Edited by E. J. West. New York, 1958.

Sixteen Self Sketches. New York, 1949.

Table-Talk of G.B.S. Edited by Archibald Henderson. New York, 1925.

About and around Shaw

Archer, William. *Henry Irving, Actor and Manager.* London [1883].

————. *The Old Drama and the New.* Boston, 1923.

————. *The Theatrical 'World' of 1895.* London, 1896.

————. *The Theatrical 'World' of 1896.* London, 1897.

————. *The Theatrical 'World' of 1897.* London, 1898.

————. and Robert W. Lowe.

"The Fashionable Tragedian," first ed. Edinburgh, 1877.

"The Fashionable Tragedian," second ed. London, 1877.

The Architectural Review, July 1898, November 1900, July 1901.

Beerbohm, Max. *Around Theatres,* 2 vols. New York, 1930.

Behrman, S. N. *Portrait of Max.* New York, 1960.

Bentley, Eric. *Bernard Shaw, 1856–1950.* New York, 1957.

————. *The Playwright as Thinker.* New York, 1946.

British Museum, Add. MSS. 50508–50743.

Chesterton, G. K. *George Bernard Shaw.* New York, 1962.

————. "George Bernard Shaw." *Fortnightly Review,* August 1931.

Clurman, Harold. *Lies Like Truth.* New York, 1960.

Coleman, John. *Memoirs of Samuel Phelps.* London, 1886.

Craig, Gordon. *Henry Irving.* New York, 1930.

————. Letter to the Editor, *The Standard,* 30 October 1905.

Crosse, Gordon. *Shakespearean Playgoing, 1890–1952.* London, 1953.

Dukore, Bernard F. *Bernard Shaw, Director.* Seattle, 1971.

Eckermann, J. P. *Conversations with Goethe.* Translated by John Oxenford; edited by J. K. Moorhead. London and New York, 1951.

Eliot, T. S. "Poetry and Drama." In *On Poetry and Poets.* London, 1957.

Ervine, St. John. *Bernard Shaw, His Life, Work, and Friends.* New York, 1956.

The Folger Shakespeare Library. Prompt copies of Charles Kean and Henry Irving.

Forbes-Robertson, Sir Johnston. *A Player Under Three Reigns.* London, 1925.

Gassner, John. "Shaw as Drama Critic." *Theatre Arts,* May 1951.

Gilbert, W. S. *The Mikado and Five Other Savoy Operas.* New York, 1961.

_____. Comment in "London Shakespeare League: Report of a public discussion on the best method of presenting Shakespeare's plays." London, 1905.

Granville Barker, Harley. "Hints on Rehearsing a Play." MS. in the British Theatre Museum Association. Quoted by permission of the Garrick Club.

_____. *Prefaces to Shakespeare,* 4 vols. London, 1963.

Guthrie, Tyrone. *A Life in the Theatre.* New York, 1959.

Harker, Joseph. *Studio and Stage.* London, 1924.

Harvard Theatre Collection. Photographs and programs.

Henderson, Archibald. *Bernard Shaw, Playboy and Prophet.* New York, 1932.

_____. *George Bernard Shaw: Man of the Century.* New York, 1956.

Irvine, William. *The Universe of G.B.S.* New York, 1949.

Irving, Laurence. *Henry Irving: The Actor and His World.* London, 1951.

Irving, Henry. *The Drama.* Boston, 1892.

_____. Advertisement in *The Literary Digest,* 14 November 1896.

James, Henry. *The Scenic Art.* Edited by Allan Wade. New Brunswick, N.J., 1948.

Kronenberger, Louis, ed. *George Bernard Shaw: A Critical Survey.* Cleveland and New York, 1953.

Lawrence, W. J. *Barry Sullivan: A Biographical Sketch.* London, 1893.

Macdonald, Dwight. "The New York Times, Alas, Alas." *Esquire,* May 1963.

Mander, Raymond, and Joe Mitchenson. *Theatrical Companion to Shaw.* London, 1954.

Meisel, Martin. *Shaw and the Nineteenth-Century Theater.* Princeton, 1963.

Montague, C. E. *Dramatic Values.* New York, 1911.

Nathan, George Jean. *Comedians All.* New York, 1919.

————. *The Critic and the Drama.* New York, 1922.

Odell, George C. D. *Shakespeare—From Betterton to Irving,* 2 vols. New York, 1963.

Pearson, Hesketh. *Beerbohm Tree, His Life and Laughter.* London, 1956.

————. *George Bernard Shaw, His Life and Personality.* New York, 1963.

————. *The Last Actor-Managers.* London, 1950.

Poel, William. *Monthly Letters.* Edited by A. M. T[rethewy]. London, 1929.

————. *Shakespeare in the Theatre.* London, 1913.

Purdom, C. B. *Harley Granville Barker.* London, 1955.

Rowell, George, ed. *Nineteenth Century Plays.* London, 1953.

Scott, Clement. *From "The Bells" to "King Arthur."* London, 1897.

————. Review of *Cymbeline. The London News,* 26 September 1896.

————. *Some Notable "Hamlets" of the Present Time.* London, 1905.

Shakespeare, *Works.* Vol. 1. Edited by Henry Irving and Frank A. Marshall. London, 1888.

————. *King Lear as Arranged for the Stage by Henry Irving.* London, 1893.

————. *King Lear at the Lyceum. Some Extracts from the Press.* London, 1893.

————. *Romeo and Juliet as Arranged for the Stage by Forbes Robertson.* London, 1895.

————. *Souvenir of King Henry VIII at the Lyceum.* London, 1892.

———. *Souvenir of King Lear at the Lyceum.* London, 1892.

"Shakespearean Recital." Two 78 rpm records, D4006 and D4007, Columbia Gramophone Co. (1928). Courtesy of Professor Frederick C. Packard, Jr., of Harvard.

Speaight, Robert. *William Poel and the Elizabethan Revival.* Cambridge, Mass., 1954.

Sprague, A. C. *Shakespearian Players and Performers.* Cambridge, Mass., 1953.

Terry, Ellen. *Memoirs.* Edited by Edith Craig and Christopher St. John. New York, 1932.

Tree, Herbert Beerbohm. *Thoughts and After-Thoughts.* London, 1913.

Tynan, Kenneth. *Curtains.* New York, 1961.

Victoria and Albert Museum. Enthoven Collection. Newspaper and magazine articles.

———. Print Room. Set designs for Charles Kean and Henry Irving.

Walkley, A. B. *Drama and Life.* London, 1907.

Wilson, Edmund. "Bernard Shaw at Eighty." In *The Triple Thinkers.* New York, 1948.

Wolff, Hellmuth Christian. *Musikgeschichte in Bildern-Oper: Szene und Darstellung von 1600 bis 1900.* Leipzig, n.d.

Yorick. "A Letter Concerning Mr. Henry Irving." Edinburgh, 1877.

Index

Achurch, Janet, 71–72, 125
Actor ("interpretative" as opposed to creative), 99–100
Actor-manager, Victorian, 69–70, 92–93
The Admirable Bashville, 27–29
Advice (Shaw's on watching a play), 122
Aeschylus, 139
All's Well That Ends Well, 58, 66, 80, 124
Alma-Tadema, Lawrence, 88
Anderson, Mary, 51
Androcles and the Lion, 19
Antony and Cleopatra, 40, 71, 119
The Apple Cart, 22, 64
Archer, William, 60, 63, 65, 97, 98, 99, 114–15, 117, 132, 151; "The Fashionable Tragedian," 98
The Architectural Review, 90
Aristotle, 149
Arms and the Man, 80, 120, 121, 144
Arnold, Matthew, 45, 51
As You Like It, 55, 78, 122, 124, 137
Ayot St. Lawrence Edition, 80, 104

Back to Methuselah, 24, 62, 84, 146
Barker, Harley Granville, 15, 20, 70, 117, 118–26, 134
Barrymore, John, 126, 134–36
Barwick, Edwin, 96
Bayreuth, 90
Beerbohm, Max, 52, 95, 117, 129, 149; Shaw had brains to scatter, 52
Beethoven, Ludwig van, 133, 141; Ninth Symphony, 108
Bennett, Arnold, 22
Benson, Frank, 91
Bentley, Eric, 37
Booth, Edwin, 93, 134

Boyer, Charles, 116
Brahms, Johannes, 37
Brecht, Bertolt, 47, 121
Brieux, Eugène, 45, 61–62, 143
Browning, Robert, 142
Bulwer Lytton, Edward, 91, 145; *Richelieu*, 15, 126, 128
Bunyan, John, 20, 32, 39, 83
Burbage, Richard, 113, 124, 126, 134
Butler, Samuel, 141, 142
Byron, Lord, 85, 142

Caesar and Cleopatra, 15, 32, 39, 77, 92, 116–17, 133, 145
Campbell, Mrs. Patrick, 20, 32, 68, 131–32
Candida, 120
Captain Brassbound's Conversion, 78, 98, 125, 126
Carlyle, Thomas, 85
Carson, Murray, 130
Cart and trumpet, 55
Cashel Byron's Profession, 28
Casson, Sir Lewis, 119, 121–23
Censorship of plays, 42–43
Cervantes, Miguel de: *Don Quixote*, 108
Chaplin, Charlie, 96
Chesterton, G. K., 55, 57, 72
Childe Roland, 95
Cibber, Colley, 90
Classic actor (Forbes Robertson as), 133
Clurman, Harold, 35, 124, 143–44, 147
Cold-water treatment in Shaw's reviews, 37. *See also* Shaw, Reviews and reviewing
Coleridge, Samuel Taylor, 51
Competition for Shaw (Shakespeare as), 13, 17

Congreve, William, 148, 150
Coriolanus, 22, 60, 88, 90, 106
Covent Garden, 89
Craig, Gordon, 92, 100, 105
Craven, Hawes, 88, 104, 133
Cromwell, Oliver, 39, 40
Crosse, Gordon, 105, 132
Cymbeline, 13, 16, 19, 29, 87, 95, 99, 100–101, 107, 133
Cymbeline Refinished, 13, 29–32

Daly, Augustin, 128–29
The Dark Lady of the Sonnets, 13, 25–27, 58, 74
Deadlines, Shaw's writing for, 138
The Devil's Disciple, 120
Dickens, Charles, 62, 81, 82, 85, 146, 151
Director, Shaw as, 118–26
The Doctor's Dilemma, 23, 120, 146
Don Juan in Hell, 41, 116, 122
Dryden, John, 54
Dukore, Bernard F.: Bernard Shaw, Director, 122
Dumas, Alexandre (père), 85, 146
Durgin-Park, 15
Duse, Eleanora, 72

Economics in Shakespeare, 18–19
Eliot, T. S., 150
Elizabethan Stage Society, 113, 117
Empress Eugénie, 99
Essays in Fabian Socialism, 18
Euripides, 85, 119, 139, 142

Fabian Society, 79, 95, 138, 140–41, 142
Farfetched Fables, 46
Fielding, Henry, 42
Filon, Augustin, 105
The Folger Shakespeare Library, 87, 106, 108
Forster, John, 151
Free tickets to the theater reviewer, 48

Galsworthy, John, 22
Garrick, David, 90, 103, 126

Gassner, John, 138
Geneva, 23
Getting Married, 74
Ghosts, origin of, 77
Gielgud, John, 91, 119, 136
Gilbert and Sullivan: Iolanthe, 134; Utopia Limited, 42
Gilbert, W. S., 113
Goethe, Johann Wolfgang von, 34, 62, 101
Goldsmith, Oliver, 151
Great Catherine, 91, 124
Guinness, Alec, 124
Guthrie, Tyrone, 92–93

Hager, Paul: opinion of Shaw's egotism, 51
Hamlet, 18, 19, 27, 29, 35, 43, 46, 50, 58, 61, 71, 73, 76–78, 79, 82, 84, 88, 90, 91, 109, 110, 120, 122, 124, 125, 126, 127, 128, 132, 133–36
Hardwicke, Cedric, 116
Harker, Joseph, 116–17
Harris, Frank, 25
Harvard, 98, 110
Harvard Theatre Collection, 98
Hauptmann, Gerhart, 119
Hazlitt, William, 82, 109, 151, 152
Heartbreak House, 24, 27, 122, 123
1 Henry IV, 17, 25, 68
Henry V, 88, 125
1 Henry VI, 32
1, 2, 3 Henry VI, 21, 55
Henry VIII, 23, 90, 110
Henry VIII, 42
Hepburn, Katharine, 126
Homer, 33, 101
Hunt, Leigh, 151
Hyde Park, 54, 55, 146
HYOMEI, 103

Ibsen, Henrik, 14, 16, 33, 35, 38, 42, 44, 53, 55, 56, 57–64, 71, 77, 79, 84, 85, 87, 91, 92, 94, 119, 125, 137–40, 142, 152; Brand, 58; A Doll's House, 15, 57–59; Emperor and Galilean, 58; Ghosts, 43, 57; Hedda Gabler,

63; *Peer Gynt*, 33, 58; *The Wild Duck*, 60, 63; discussion a theatrical novelty, 139; pessimism and lack of humor, 62–63; spectators made persons of drama, 58, 139
Immaturity, 17
Income, Shaw's and Shakespeare's, 18
"In Good King Charles's Golden Days," 23
The Intelligent Woman's Guide to Socialism and Capitalism, 19, 140
The Irrational Knot, 84, 140
Irving, Henry, 15, 16, 87–112, 114, 115–16, 118, 120, 126, 127, 128, 130, 134, 136, 151–52; "Bardicide," practiced by him at Lyceum Theatre, 14–15, 87; cuts in Shakespeare, 105–8; endorsed cold remedy, 103; lacked literary sense, 15, 107; picturesque actor (description of him by Henry James), 102; recordings of, 110; Shaw's jealousy of, 95

James, Henry, 101–2; his description of Irving as picturesque actor, 102
Jitta's Atonement, 61
John Bull's Other Island, 120
Johnson, Samuel, 49
Julius Caesar, 68, 133

Kean, Charles, 87, 88, 104, 110, 129
Kean, Edmund, 109, 126, 151
Keats, John, 82
Kierkegaard, Sören, 125
King John, 65, 135
King Lear, 16, 17, 19, 27, 29, 33–34, 35, 62, 76, 90, 98, 100, 104–7, 119

Labor Party, 140
Lamb, Charles, 151
La Rochefoucauld, François, 65, 142
Laughton, Charles, 116
Lewes, George Henry, 151
Lowe, Robert W.: "The Fashionable Tragedian," 98
Lyceum Theatre, 15, 53, 87–113, 115, 123, 133

Macbeth, 17, 20, 22, 76, 78, 90, 119, 124, 125, 132
"Macbeth. A Novel," 21, 22
Macdonald, Dwight, 65
Macready, William Charles, 104, 111, 126
Maeterlinck, Maurice, 119
Major Barbara, 80, 84, 120
Man and Superman, 34, 41, 77, 81, 82–83, 116, 120, 122, 148–49; *Don Juan in Hell*, 41, 116, 122
Manchester Guardian, 88
Mander, Raymond, and Mitchenson, Joe: *Theatrical Companion to Shaw*, 80
The Man of Destiny, 15, 93
Marlowe, Christopher, 30; *Doctor Faustus*, 118
Marx, Karl, 64, 141, 142; *Das Kapital*, 65
Measure for Measure, 18, 58, 78, 80, 82, 111, 112
Meisel, Martin, 44
The Merchant of Venice, 87, 88, 98, 104, 111
The Merry Wives of Windsor, 60, 73
Meyerbeer, Giacomo, 141; *Robert le Diable*, 89
A Midsummer Night's Dream, 59, 67, 115, 116, 119, 128–29
The Millionairess, 126
Milton, John, 39
Misalliance, 18
Mitchenson, Joe. *See* Mander, Raymond
Molière, 62, 146, 148, 150; *Le Festin de Pierre*, 33
Montague, C. E., 88, 117–18
Montaigne, Michel de, 143
Moorehead, Agnes, 116
Mrs Warren's Profession, 42, 44
Mozart, Wolfgang Amadeus, 56, 68, 86, 109, 137, 150; *Don Giovanni*, 33, 41, 148–49; *The Marriage of Figaro*, 71
Much Ado About Nothing, 55, 70, 71, 82, 89, 97, 98, 106, 113

Murray, Gilbert, 119
Music: imaginative safety-valve for Shaw, 72; transmuted into literature, 148
My Fair Lady, 147

Nathan, George Jean, 49, 50
National Theatre, 25–27
Newman, Ernest, 36
New York Times, 65
Nietzsche, Friedrich, 141, 142
Nobel Prize, Shaw's, 63

O'Flaherty V.C., 22
Olivier, Laurence, 76, 93, 97, 124, 136
Operatic scenic peep-show stage, 110
Originality in Shaw, 16; in testing creeds and codes, 140–44; in dramatic technique, 144–48
Othello, 24, 45, 70, 73–76, 98, 109, 115, 125, 126
Our Theatres in the Nineties, 42, 55
Overplaying, Shaw's encouragement of, 120–21
Overruled, 43, 44

Packard, Frederick C., Jr., 110
Parables, Shaw's plays as, 44–45
Parodies: of *Macbeth*, 22; of music reviewing, 50; of Ibsen club, 60; of Shaw, 79
Passmore, Walter, Esq., 96
Pearson, Hesketh, 17, 61, 120, 130
The Perfect Wagnerite, 40
Pericles, 55
Phelps, Samuel, 88, 93, 104
The Philanderer, 60
Plautus, 145–46
Poel, William, 15, 21, 105, 110–19, 136
Press Cuttings, 42
Prince of Entertainers (Shakespeare as), 119
Problem play, 58–59
Prompt copies: of *Major Barbara*, 80; of Shakespeare plays, 106
Propaganda, art subservient to, 46

Prose style (Shaw's described by T. S. Eliot), 150
Purdom, C. B., 119, 120
Pygmalion, 67, 71, 84, 92, 131, 151; (*My Fair Lady*), 147

The Quintessence of Ibsenism, 57, 58, 74, 93, 138

Redgrave, Michael, 124
Rehearsal notes of director, 124–26
Rewriting, practiced by Shakespeare, 29
Richard II, 65, 88, 112, 119, 129
Richard III, 65, 76, 97, 110, 111
Robertson, Forbes, 15, 75, 89, 92, 116, 126, 128, 132–34, 136; *A Player Under Three Reigns*, 89
Romeo and Juliet, 65, 69, 88, 97, 131–32
Royal Court Theatre, 80, 109, 119
Ruskin, John, 85

Saint Joan, 32, 35, 78, 116, 118, 121, 123
Sardou, Victorien: *Madame sans Gêne*, 93
The Saturday Review, 13, 29, 33, 45, 66, 138
Schnitzler, Arthur, 119
Scott, Clement, 52, 87, 105, 132
Scott, Dixon, 46
Scott, Sir Walter, 72, 85, 101, 146
Sensuousness in art, Shaw's objection to, 39–40; Shaw's susceptibility to, 40–41
Shakespeare, John, 18
Shakespeare, William:
All's Well That Ends Well, 58, 66, 80, 124
Antony and Cleopatra, 40, 71, 119
As You Like It, 55, 78, 122, 124, 137
Coriolanus, 22, 60, 88, 90, 106
Cymbeline, 13, 16, 19, 29, 87, 95, 99, 100–101, 107, 133
Hamlet, 18, 19, 27, 29, 35, 43, 46, 50, 58, 61, 71, 73, 76–78, 79, 82, 84, 88, 90, 91, 109, 110, 120, 122,

124, 125, 126, 127, 128, 132, 133–36
1 Henry IV, 17, 25, 68
Henry V, 88, 125
1 Henry VI, 32
1, 2, 3 Henry VI, 21, 55
Henry VIII, 23, 90, 110
Julius Caesar, 68, 133
King John, 65, 135
King Lear, 16, 17, 19, 27, 29, 33–34, 35, 62, 76, 90, 98, 100, 104–7, 119
Macbeth, 17, 20, 22, 76, 78, 90, 119, 124, 125, 132
Measure for Measure, 18, 58, 78, 80, 82, 111, 112
The Merchant of Venice, 87, 88, 98, 104, 111
The Merry Wives of Windsor, 60, 73
A Midsummer Night's Dream, 59, 67, 115, 116, 119, 128–29
Much Ado About Nothing, 55, 70, 71, 82, 89, 97, 98, 106, 113
Othello, 24, 45, 70, 73–76, 98, 109, 115, 125, 126
Pericles, 55
Richard II, 65, 88, 112, 119, 129
Richard III, 65, 76, 97, 110, 111
Romeo and Juliet, 65, 69, 88, 97, 131–32
Sonnets, 20, 25–26, 57
The Tempest, 111, 113–16
Timon of Athens, 55
Titus Andronicus, 55
Troilus and Cressida, 33, 58, 80
Twelfth Night, 43, 67, 109, 111, 113, 119, 130
Two Gentlemen of Verona, 129
The Winter's Tale, 88, 119
Shakes Versus Shav, 13, 17, 27
Shaw, Charlotte, 20, 61
Shaw, George Bernard:
    The Admirable Bashville, 27–29
    Androcles and the Lion, 19
    The Apple Cart, 22, 64
    Arms and the Man, 80, 120, 121, 144

Back to Methuselah, 24, 62, 84, 146
Caesar and Cleopatra, 15, 32, 39, 77, 92, 116–17, 133, 145
Candida, 120
Captain Brassbound's Conversion, 78, 98, 125, 126
Cashel Byron's Profession, 28
Cymbeline Refinished, 13, 29–32
The Dark Lady of the Sonnets, 13, 25–27, 58, 74
The Devil's Disciple, 120
The Doctor's Dilemma, 23, 120, 146
Don Juan in Hell, 41, 116, 122
Essays in Fabian Socialism, 18
Farfetched Fables, 46
Geneva, 23
Getting Married, 74
Great Catherine, 91, 124
Heartbreak House, 24, 27, 122, 123
Immaturity, 17
"In Good King Charles's Golden Days," 23
The Intelligent Woman's Guide to Socialism and Capitalism, 19, 140
The Irrational Knot, 84, 140
Jitta's Atonement, 61
John Bull's Other Island, 120
"Macbeth. A Novel," 21, 22
Major Barbara, 80, 84, 120
Man and Superman, 34, 41, 77, 81, 82–83, 116, 120, 122, 148–49; *Don Juan in Hell*, 41, 116, 122
The Man of Destiny, 15, 93
The Millionairess, 126
Misalliance, 18
Mrs Warren's Profession, 42, 44
O'Flaherty V.C., 22
Our Theatres in the Nineties, 42, 55
Overruled, 43, 44
The Perfect Wagnerite, 40
The Philanderer, 60
Press Cuttings, 42
Pygmalion, 67, 71, 84, 92, 131, 151; (*My Fair Lady*), 147
The Quintessence of Ibsenism, 57, 58, 74, 93, 138

Saint Joan, 32, 35, 78, 116, 118, 121, 123

Shakes Versus Shav, 13, 17, 27

The Shewing-Up of Blanco Posnet, 42

"The Theatre of the Future," 21

Three Plays for Puritans, 32, 39, 40, 54, 112, 141

An Unsocial Socialist, 78

Widowers' Houses, 118, 138

You Never Can Tell, 22, 120

Shaw, reviews and reviewing: cold-water treatment in the reviews, 37; his power as reviewer of Shakespeare, 14; reviewing *Cymbeline,* 100–101; his unfairness, 51, 57

Shaw's characteristics: cap and bells irresistible to him, 60; jealousy of Irving, 95; modesty alien to his temperament, 54, 100; motivation of his Shakespearean criticism, 36–37; platform style, 55; snort, 150; vegetarianism, 51

Shaw's cook: her theatrical opinion, 125

Shaw's descent from Shakespeare, 17

Shaw's education and Shakespeare's, 18

Shaw's opinions: on average young University graduate, 52–53; "Bardicide," practiced by Henry Irving at Lyceum Theatre, 14–15, 87; blank verse, "so childishly easy and expeditious," 28; crime not interesting, 118; on cuts in Shakespeare by Irving, 105–8; discussion a theatrical novelty in Ibsen, 139; ditch-water and fresh paint (*A Doll's House* and *A Midsummer Night's Dream*), 59; God's jokes, the world as only one of (to Tolstoy), 34; ideas preferred to passions, 75; imagination in viewing a play, 113–14; movies, objection to morality of, 38; murder, actor should commit, 118; opera, Shakespeare like, 66, 89; platitudinous fudge ("To

be or not to be"), 61; plot the ruin of a story, 151; plumber (Hamlet's experiences simply could not have happened to a), 126

Shaw, George Carr, 18

Shaw, Lucy, 19

Sheridan, Richard Brinsley, 92, 122, 148, 149

The Shewing-Up of Blanco Posnet, 42

Sidney, Sir Philip, 51

Sonnets, 20, 25–26, 57

Sophocles, 139; *Oedipus the King,* 58, 125, 135

Speaight, Robert, 110, 112

Spectators. See Ibsen

Stage: as mirror, 43–44, 58; directions, 79–81; history, studying is tantalizing and frustrating, 15; management, 122, *see* Advice; scenery, 15, 66–67, 87–91, 95, 97, 104–5, 108, 111–12, 116–17, 119, 133; silence on, 123, 133

Stanford, Dr., 49

The Star, 13, 94

Strauss, Richard: *Elektra,* 36–37

Strindberg, August, 62, 63–64

Sullivan, Arthur, 109

Sullivan, Barry, 15, 96, 120, 126–28, 134, 136

Swinburne, Algernon, 21

Tate, Nahum, 90, 106

The Tempest, 111, 113–16

Tennyson, Alfred Lord, 91, 98, 115

Terence, 145–46

Terry, Ellen, 15, 16, 68, 95–101, 103, 107, 120, 126, 127, 131, 133; *Memoirs,* 98–99; described slope of women, 99

"The Theatre of the Future," 21

Three Plays for Puritans, 32, 39, 40, 54, 112, 141

The Times, 65, 149

Timon of Athens, 55

Titus Andronicus, 55

Tolstoy, Leo, 29, 34
Translation, Shaw's threatened of *Hamlet*, 61
Translations, William Archer's of Ibsen, 60
Trebitsch, Siegfried, 61
Tree, Herbert Beerbohm, 91, 92, 120, 126, 128–31
Troilus and Cressida, 33, 58, 80
Tussaud, Madame, 88
Twain, Mark: *Huckleberry Finn*, 23
Twelfth Night, 43, 67, 109, 111, 113, 119, 130
Two Gentlemen of Verona, 129
Tynan, Kenneth, 35

An Unsocial Socialist, 78

Vedrenne, J. E., 119
Verdi, Giuseppe, 150; *Don Carlos*, 89; *Falstaff* and *Otello*, 73; *Il Trovatore*, 148
Victoria and Albert Museum, 87
Villains, 74, 75–76
Visconti, Luchino, 89

Wagner, Richard, 54, 56, 90, 101, 121, 137, 146; *Ring of the Nibelungen*, 33, 40, 71; *Tristan und Isolde*, 65, 69
Walkley, A. B., 65, 117, 149
Walpole, Robert, 42
Webster, John, 58
Widowers' Houses, 118, 138
Wilde, Oscar, 46, 85, 142, 149
Wilson, Edmund: "Bernard Shaw at Eighty," 47–48
The Winter's Tale, 88, 119
Wolff, Hellmuth Christian: *Musikgeschichte in Bildern–Oper: Szene und Darstellung von 1600 bis 1900*, 89
Woman, Shaw's like Shakespeare's, 77–78
Women. *See* Ellen Terry
Word-music, 14, 65–75, 85–86, 137
The World, 13, 60
Wright, Frank Lloyd: *The Future of Architecture*, 53–54
Writers of the first and second order, 84–85, 140

Yeats, William Butler, 119
Yorick, 98
You Never Can Tell, 22, 120